CLIGÈS

CHRÉTIEN DE TROYES

CLIGÈS

Translated by

RUTH HARWOOD CLINE

THE UNIVERSITY OF GEORGIA PRESS
Athens & London

© 2000 by the University of Georgia Press

Athens, Georgia 30602

All rights reserved

Set in 11/14 Centaur by Walton Harris

Printed and bound by Maple-Vail

The paper in this book meets the guidelines for

permanence and durability of the Committee on

Production Guidelines for Book Longevity of the

Council on Library Resources.

Printed in the United States of America

00 01 02 03 04 C 5 4 3 2 1

00 01 02 03 04 P 5 4 3 2 1

Library of Congress Cataloging-in-Publication Data

Chrétien, de Troyes, 12th cent.

[Cligès. English]

Cligès / Chrétien de Troyes ; translated by Ruth Harwood Cline.

p. cm.

Includes bibliographical references.

ISBN 0-8203-2147-8 (alk. paper). — ISBN 0-8203-2142-7 (pbk. : alk. paper)

1. Romances—Translations into English.

2. Knights and knighthood—Romances.

3. Civilization, Medieval—Romances.

4. Arthurian romances.

I. Cline, Ruth Harwood.   II. Title.

PQ1445.C5E5   2000

841'.1—dc21   99-30723

British Library Cataloging-in-Publication Data available

CONTENTS

ACKNOWLEDGMENTS

Chrétien de Troyes was not well known to English readers when I began to translate *Yvain; or, The Knight with the Lion* in 1969. I was one of a group of native English speakers who had majored in French language and literature and progressed to Old French in graduate school. Chrétien was highly esteemed in that circle, but it was not a large one. As a Smith student who took courses during her senior year at Barnard College, I studied with Professor Patricia Terry, a gifted translator of Old French lays. I felt that her verse form of rhymed iambic tetrameter would be a suitable and effective way of translating Chrétien's romances into English. In this way a thirty-year project began.

Professional translators must be able to express the underlying layer of meaning in the source language while having the confidence to be idiomatic in the target language. They know that they can convey only part of the original, but they convey a very large portion of both form and substance. Moreover, they know how to select what is most important. Their work is accurate, polished, and idiomatic. Their translations can stand alone or alongside the source material. They know how to walk along the border of two languages, as if they were on Hadrian's Wall. The footing is irregular, but the view on both sides is magnificent.

This book marks the completion of my effort to translate all five of Chrétien's romances. On this occasion, I wish to express my deepest appreciation to my colleagues in the American Translators Association, who awarded me the Louis Galantière Prize for the best non-German literary translation published in the United States between 1990 and 1992 for *Lancelot*. Their recognition has sustained and encouraged me to complete my translations of the works of Chrétien de Troyes.

I am particularly grateful for the steadfast love and support of my husband, William R. Cline, throughout this decades-long venture. Our daughters, Alison Cline Earles and Marian Cline le Grelle, have heartened me by their interest and encouragement in my work from the perspective of their adult lives.

Professor Jo Ann Moran Cruz, chair of the Department of History of Georgetown University, has been my friend and adviser for over twenty-five years. Her recommendation and encouragement were critical in my decision to enter a doctoral program in medieval history at Georgetown. Jo Ann is noted for her penetrating intellect and excellent publications, but also for her generosity, energy, and enthusiasm. She has used my translations of Chrétien de Troyes for many years and has praised their effectiveness in the classroom. She took time from her overwhelming schedule to read and comment upon the manuscripts of *Erec and Enide* and *Cligès*. I dedicate *Cligès* to my friend Jo Ann Hoeppner Moran Cruz in gratitude.

INTRODUCTION

Chrétien de Troyes created the Arthurian romance as a literary genre in the latter part of the twelfth century. He was the first to write long love stories in Old French verse about King Arthur and his knights. *Cligès* follows *Erec and Enide* and was probably written around 1176. These two romances are among Chrétien's earliest works. Although they are not as polished as his *Yvain; or, The Knight with the Lion* or as famous as his *Lancelot; or, The Knight of the Cart* and *Perceval; or, The Story of the Grail*, they are interesting and important. They contain many clues to the identity of the author and demonstrate his familiarity with the England of Henry II. In *Erec*, Chrétien demonstrates the art of turning an adventure story into a literary masterpiece. He establishes the plot structure of his future romances and develops the rhetorical technique of detailed description. In *Cligès*, Chrétien begins his reworkings of the Tristan legend. His writing style is far more complex and enlivened by word play, Ovidian love monologues, and rhetorical topoi. In both works he synthesizes romantic love with marriage. The evolution of his literary skills over the course of these early romances is critical to an understanding and appreciation of the polish and subtlety of his mature works.

The birth and death dates of Chrétien de Troyes are unknown but thought to fall between 1135 and 1191. *Erec and Enide* was probably written around 1170. In the prologue to *Cligès*, after referring to *Erec and Enide*, Chrétien mentions other works. They include a lost vernacular rendering of Ovid's *Art of Love*, *The Amores*, and *Cures for Love* and two Ovidian tales: a lost version of the Pelops legend that he calls *The Shoulder Bite* and a tale of the metamorphosis of hoopoe, swallow, and nightingale that is known as *Philomena*.[1] He also wrote a version of the Tristan legend called *King Mark and Fair Isolde*. This work, which has been lost, would have been one of the earliest versions of the Tristan legend; it probably preceded the *Tristan* of Thomas d'Angleterre (c. 1172–1176) and of Béroul (late twelfth century; dated 1165–1190, but more probably written after 1190).[2] His third and fourth romances, *Lancelot; or, The Knight of the Cart* and *Yvain; or, The Knight with the Lion*, are dated c. 1177–1179. *Lancelot*, dedicated to the Countess Marie of Champagne, was completed by the clerk Godefroi de Leigny (Lagny) at Chrétien's direction. *Yvain* is set in the forest of Paimpont/Brocéliande in Brittany and seems to have been written concurrently with *Lancelot*.[3] *Perceval; or, The Story of the Grail* was probably started between 1179 and 1181.[4] According to the continuator Gerbert de Montreuil, writing between 1226 and 1230, Chrétien died leaving *Perceval* unfinished.[5] Philip of Flanders died in 1191.[6] Chrétien also wrote two love songs.[7] Chrétien de Troyes may be the same Chrétien who wrote *Guillaume d'Angleterre* (*William of England*), a short religious romance of about three thousand verses without an Arthurian theme, set in Norfolk.[8] *Philomena* and *Guillaume* are not considered to be masterpieces. Chrétien's literary reputation is based upon his five romances, particularly *Lancelot* and *Perceval*. They are the earliest known versions of the love affair between Lancelot and Guinevere and the Quest of the Grail and inspired numerous adaptations and continuations. Malory, Chaucer, Tennyson, and Wagner, among others, are successors of Chrétien de Troyes.

Many questions have been raised about Chrétien de Troyes and this earlier period of his literary career when he wrote *Erec* and *Cligès*. Was he also the Chrétien who wrote *Guillaume d'Angleterre*? How did he obtain the factual information about England and Windsor Castle contained in *Cligès*? Did the Ovidian adaptations and Tristan story that he mentions in the prologue of *Cligès* precede or follow *Erec*? Internal clues in his works suggest that Chrétien de Troyes was an educated aristocrat in holy orders and that he had connections to the court of Henry II of England (r. 1154–1189). Since Chrétien scholars agree with regard to his association with Count Henri (1127–1181) and Countess Marie (1145–1198) of Champagne when he wrote *Lancelot* (c. 1177), it is possible to work backward from the late 1170s to suggest ways their kinship network might have served Chrétien in his earlier years and to shed light on these questions.

The map of Europe in 1170 was very different from that of its present nation states. After William, duke of Normandy, conquered England in 1066, England and Normandy were under the control of the English king. England was devastated by a civil war during the reign of King Stephen (r. 1135–1154). Stephen was the nephew of William's son Henry I (r. 1100–1135) and the uncle of the count of Champagne. Henry of Anjou, the grandson of Henry I, succeeded his cousin Stephen in 1154. Because of his brilliant marriage to Eleanor of Aquitaine, the former queen of the French king Louis VII (b. c. 1120, r. 1137–1180), and his conquest of independent Brittany, Henry II of England controlled western France from Flanders to Spain by 1170. Modern Belgium and part of northern France were ruled by Philip, count of Flanders. Louis VII, king of France, ruled the small territory of Ile de France around Paris. Louis VII had dealt for years with the illustrious father of the count of Champagne, Count Thibaut "the Great" IV of Blois and II of Champagne (b. c. 1093, r. Blois and Champagne jointly 1125–1152). Thibaut's mother, Adela, was the sister of the English king Henry I. Upon Thibaut's death in 1152, his extensive lands south and east of Ile de France were divided among his older sons. Count Henri received Champagne, and Count Thibaut V received Blois. The Holy Roman Emperor, Frederick Barbarossa, controlled the region now occupied by Germany, Austria, and northern Italy. One of his most rebellious liegemen was Henry the Lion, duke of Saxony. Modern Greece, Turkey (including Constantinople, now Istanbul), and part of the Middle East were ruled by Emperor Manuel Comnenus (c. 1122–1180, r. 1143–1180).

Louis VII was eager to ally his small territory of Ile de France with the vast neighboring territories of Blois and Champagne, and he cultivated Thibaut's sons. Count Henri (1127–1181) accompanied Louis VII and Eleanor of Aquitaine on the Second Crusade, where he was knighted at age twenty by Emperor Manuel Comnenus at Constantinople in 1147. Eleanor of Aquitaine left her daughters Marie, age seven, and Alix, under age two, with Louis VII when their marriage was annulled in 1152.[9] Marie was betrothed to Count Henri by 1153 and placed in the convent of Avenay in Champagne for instruction.[10] Louis VII appointed Count Henri's younger brother, Count Thibaut V of Blois, seneschal of France and betrothed him to Marie's younger sister, Alix.[11] Both marriages probably took place around 1164 when Marie was nineteen and Alix was fourteen years old. When Louis VII was widowed in 1160, he had an opportunity for a third alliance and married the youngest sister of Count Henri. Adele (1140–1206) became the mother of Louis's heir, Philip Augustus (b. 1165, r. 1180–1223). By 1170 the House of Blois-Champagne, which had often been allied by ties of kinship with England and Normandy at the beginning of the twelfth century, was firmly linked to Louis VII and France by three marriages that took place in the 1160s.

Troyes, the seat of the count of Champagne, was a cosmopolitan place and an important trading center.[12] Goods and information from all over the known world flowed through the four annual fairs of Champagne, one of which was held at Troyes and another at Lagny. Count Henri, a crusader and a fine administrator, was a handsome, well-educated nobleman known as "the Liberal" for his wealth and generosity. When Chrétien de Troyes wrote *Cligès* (c. 1176), Count

Henri was almost fifty years old. He and his much younger wife, Countess Marie, were noted literary patrons. On his father's side, Count Henri was directly descended from Charlemagne and William the Conqueror.[13] Count Henri's paternal uncles were King Stephen of England (b. c. 1097, r. 1135–1154) and Henry (c. 1099–1171), bishop of Winchester (1129) and abbot of Glastonbury (1126). Count Henri was the second cousin of Stephen's successor, Henry II, whose wife, Eleanor of Aquitaine, was the count's mother-in-law. On his mother's side, Count Henri was half German; he was the oldest of ten children born of his father's marriage to Mathilda of Carinthia in 1123.[14] Champagne bordered on the Holy Roman Empire, and Count Henri occasionally engaged in diplomacy with the German emperor.[15] Thus the personal connections of the count and countess of Champagne extended from England across the Holy Roman Empire to Constantinople.[16]

The court of Champagne had particularly close ties to England through Count Henri's uncle Henry and two of his brothers, Guillaume and Hugh. All three had lived in England and traveled back and forth to France before 1170. These kinsmen lived in places mentioned in the works of Chrétien de Troyes.

After the coronation of Henry II, the count's uncle Henry, bishop of Winchester and abbot of Glastonbury, left England in 1155 for France. He stayed at the abbey of Cluny until 1162, although he visited England briefly in 1159. He returned to attend the consecration of Thomas à Becket as archbishop of Canterbury in 1162 and died at about age seventy at Winchester on 8 August 1171. Subsequently, Winchester and Glastonbury Abbey were considered to be the sites of King Arthur's court, Round Table, and grave.

A younger brother of Count Henri, known as Guillaume aux Blanches Mains (William of the white hands) (1135–1202), spent his early teens in England in the care of his uncle Henry, bishop of Winchester.[17] Guillaume returned to France in 1151 and embarked on a distinguished career in the church.[18] By 1170 Guillaume had been bishop of Chartres (1165), archbishop of Sens (1168), and papal legate in England (1168–1170).[19] Like Count Henri and Countess Marie, Guillaume was also a prominent literary patron.[20] He would rise to greater heights in the church.[21]

In addition, Count Henri had a natural half brother named Hugh, who was probably born well before their father's marriage in 1123. While many natural sons were destined for the church, Thibaut the Great raised Hugh as a knight.

Described as noble, manly, and energetic in his bearing, Hugh was badly wounded in war. During his convalescence at Tiron Abbey near Chartres, Hugh underwent a religious conversion and became a monk of that eremitical congregation. Tiron Abbey had longstanding ties with the British Isles dating to its foundation between 1109 and 1114 by the hermit Bernard of Abbeville.[22] Through the influence of his uncles, King Stephen and Bishop Henry, in 1146 Hugh became abbot of St. Benet of Holme in Norfolk, an abbey with close reciprocal ties to the abbey of Bury St. Edmund's.[23] Subsequently Hugh was abbot of Chertsey near Windsor from 1150 to 1163.[24] After Stephen's death and Henry II's accession in 1154, Hugh returned to France and, with Count Henri's help, was elected abbot of Lagny, outside Paris, in 1163.[25] Hugh probably died in 1171.[26] The kinship associations with Norfolk, Bury St. Edmund's, Windsor, and Lagny show a remarkable coincidence with places described by Chrétien in *Guillaume d'Angleterre* and *Cligès* and the birth place of the clerk Godefroi of Lagny who completed *Lancelot*.

This kinship network of the House of Blois-Champagne was in place when Chrétien began to write his romances. Abbot Hugh was reunited with Count Henri in Champagne around 1155 and was abbot of Lagny from 1163 to 1171. Bishop Henry had returned to Winchester. Thibaut V of Blois, as royal seneschal, dealt with Henry II on the Continent. Guillaume aux Blanches Mains as archbishop of Sens and papal legate in England was negotiating the Becket case. The clergymen were the family members who had resided in England and were familiar with British geography. Even if the poet never traveled from his native country, the kinship network of the House of Blois-Champagne could account for the transmission of the matter of Britain to Chrétien de Troyes.

With regard to the questions about the poet's early career, the existence of Count Henri's half brother, Abbot Hugh of Lagny, is a new argument to support the contention that the Chrétien who wrote *Guillaume d'Angleterre* was actually Chrétien de Troyes. Abbot Hugh could have furnished information about Norfolk. The abbey of Bury St. Edmund with the shrine of St. Edmund, a Christian Saxon king martyred by the Danes, was the greatest place of pilgrimage in England until Becket was martyred at Canterbury. Chrétien might have visited it in the entourage of one of Count Henri's relatives in England. Chrétien claims to have obtained the source for *Guillaume* from the library of that monastery.[27] According to legend, St. Edmund was shot with arrows and beheaded.

One of his emblems is the wolf that allegedly guarded his head after his death. In *Guillaume*, a wolf carries away one of King Guillaume's twin sons and leaves him to be adopted by merchants. They name the child Lovel after the wolf. The structure and themes of *Guillaume*, particularly that of religious conversion, are paralleled in the works of Chrétien de Troyes. Since the name Chrétien was rare, it seems unlikely that there would have been two poets by that name writing for a court with specific Norfolk connections.

If Chrétien de Troyes and the Chrétien who wrote *Guillaume d'Angleterre* are the same man, I suggest that the work was a youthful exercise in unified plotting and innovative verse forms. Chrétien says in the prologue to *Guillaume* that he intends to tell a story using various verse forms: rhyme, consonance, or leonine verse (in the leonine verse form, a word rhyming with the end rhyme is placed before the caesura). Chrétien will not add or omit anything and will not bring in another story, that is, he intends to write a single, unified work. Chrétien de Troyes did use rhymes ranging in complexity from infrequent assonance and consonance to *rime riche* (perfect two-syllable rhymes) and *annominatio* (words with the same form but different meanings). He introduced such innovations as breaking the couplet and enjambment.[28] The style of *Guillaume* is very similar to *Erec*, and both works are written in a style that is much less complex than that of Chrétien de Troyes's four later romances. Lindvall's stylistic analysis consistently situates *Guillaume* as being written by Chrétien de Troyes and closer to *Erec* than to *Cligès*.[29] This religious and ancestral romance seems to be an early work by Chrétien de Troyes, written during his period of experimentation with new verse forms and organized plot structure, the *conjointure* mentioned in *Erec*.

It is uncertain why Chrétien chose not to mention *Guillaume* in the prologue to *Cligès*. Perhaps the outbreak of hostilities in the years 1173 and 1174 was a consideration. Eleanor of Aquitaine and her sons revolted against Henry II in alliance with Louis VII and the count of Champagne. Henry II put down the revolt, imprisoned Eleanor in England, and disbanded her court in Poitiers. If Chrétien had been associated with the English court, he had probably returned to Troyes by that time.

Instead of obtaining British material through the court kinship network, Chrétien de Troyes might also have obtained factual information about England if he had spent some time at a Plantagenet court and visited England early in his literary career. One possibility, supported by matching Chrétien's place names with the itinerary of Henry II, is that Chrétien de Troyes might have been in the entourage of Henry II and Geoffrey, duke of Brittany, at Rennes in May 1169 and at Nantes on Christmas of that year. Subsequently Chrétien might have followed Henry II to England during April and May 1170.[30] As Bullock-Davies proposes, Chrétien might have landed at the port of Bitterne Manor below Southampton on the double high tide that occurs in late midafternoon in May. From the port he might have ridden the twelve miles to Winchester, the seat of Count Henri's uncle, Bishop Henry. He might have attended the coronation of Henry the Young King, which inspired him to include the image of the leopards of Henry II's coat of arms in his description of Erec's chair. Possibly with Henry, bishop of Winchester, or Henry the Young King Chrétien might have proceeded the twenty-five miles from London via Staines and Slough to Windsor Castle. There he would have seen the drought, the Thames low with its gravel bank easily forded, and tents on Datchet Mead, as they are described in *Cligès*. He would have found Windsor Castle undergoing major construction of its defensive works: the wooden palisades were being replaced by a stone wall, the great stone tower was being built, and the middle and low wards or baileys were being walled in by three walls.[31] As a literary and strategic exercise, Chrétien might have planned a successful invasion of Windsor Castle from the perspective of the upper ward, where the royal apartments were located.[32] During such a stay, Chrétien would have seen the royal regalia and "sterlings blanch" he describes in Erec's coronation. He would have learned the geography of southern England, including the route of the royal messengers to the Continent via London, Canterbury, and Dover.[33] He would have learned of Henry II's friend Brian of the Isles and of the tourney ground at Wallingford.[34] This visit would have given him the detailed information about England that is echoed in *Erec* and *Cligès*. It is not implausible that Chrétien was in the entourage of one of the count's clerical relatives or a visitor at the court of the English king.

The last question about Chrétien's early literary career is whether the Ovidian adaptations and Tristan story mentioned in the prologue of *Cligès* preceded or followed *Erec*. The literary style of Chrétien de Troyes changed considerably between the time he completed his first romance, *Erec and Enide*, probably shortly after 1170, and the time he began his second romance, *Cligès*, probably around 1176. One new and important influence was Ovid, particularly *The Amores, The Art of Love*, and the *Metamorphoses*.[35] Chrétien took from Ovid the image of love as a god called Love or Cupid with a bow and a quiver full of arrows, whose tormented victims are inspired to debate their feelings in lengthy love monologues. In *Erec*, the love between the couple is inspired by their physical beauty and expressed by their physical joy. They seldom analyze their feelings; Enide's emotional state is most often expressed by floods of tears of joy or grief. *Cligès* contains lengthy love monologues with intricate word play, often on the same key words. It also contains four monologues reproaching Death, with three following each other in rapid succession, whereas *Erec* only contains one. *Lancelot* and his subsequent romances contain love monologues and reproaches of Death, but they are written with more skill and restraint. In *Cligès*, Chrétien adopts new rhetorical devices. In *Erec* Chrétien displays familiarity with the rhetorical portrait, mirror, and nature topoi. In *Cligès*, he introduces the topoi of the passage of learning from the ancient to the modern world, the string of impossibilities, the world turned upside down, and the paradoxical incompleteness of love without fear.[36] One explanation for this change in literary style may be that he was still young and experimenting and perfecting his writing skills. Another explanation may lie in the list of his works in the prologue of *Cligès*.

The chronology of these works by Chrétien is disputed. The most widely accepted theory is that Chrétien listed his works in reverse chronological order in the prologue of *Cligès*, i.e., that he began his literary career by writing adaptations of Ovid and one of the earliest versions of the Tristan story and then wrote *Erec*, which contains some references to Tristan and Ovidian material.[37] Nonetheless, the lost *Shoulder Bite* and the surviving *Philomena* reflect Chrétien's immersion in Ovid's *Metamorphoses*, particularly book 6. The unhappy lovers therein as well as the opening of *The Amores* were fresh in his memory when he wrote *Cligès* around 1176. Soredamors's love monologue about Alexander's handsomeness is inspired by Medea's monologue about Jason in book 7. Thus the Ovidian references in *Philomena* raise the possibility that it was written after *Erec* (around 1170) and closer to *Cligès* (around 1176).

The influence of Wace and Thomas, who wrote for the Plantagenet court, also supports this chronology. Chrétien was familiar with Wace's *Roman de Brut*, completed in 1155. Hoepffner notes that *Philomena* and *Erec* were about equally influenced by *Brut*, followed by *Cligès*. Subsequently the influence of Wace diminishes and almost completely disappears in the later romances.[38] The last two parts of Wace's *Roman de Rou*, a verse history of the dukes of Normandy begun in 1160, are dated 1170-1174. This section contains the memorable lines about what Wace considered to be his foolish visit to the Fountain of Barenton in Brittany and his futile attempt to cause rainfall by pouring water on the stone. Chrétien repeats these lines in *Philomena* and in *Yvain*.[39] Schulze-Busacker notes that *Philomena* has five Anglo-Norman proverbs in common with Wace's *Rou*.[40] Chrétien may have used a Provençal or poetic source for his lost *King Mark and Fair Isolde*. His few references to Tristan in *Erec* are not taken from Thomas's *Tristan*, which is now dated 1172–1176.[41] *Cligès* seems written in reaction to Thomas's *Tristan* and contains severe criticism of the adulterous love affair.[42] Clearly Chrétien was influenced by the works written by these English court writers in the early 1170s.

Thus I suggest Chrétien concentrated on British materials prior to 1173 or 1174, when he wrote the lost *King Mark and Fair Isolde, Erec,* and *Guillaume*. At the Plantagenet courts, he became familiar with the *Roman de Rou* of Wace and the *Tristan* of Thomas d'Angleterre. The love songs, which refer to Tristan and to the Ovidian god of love, may have been written while Eleanor was at Poitiers. Toward the end of this transitional period between *Erec* and *Cligès*, Chrétien immersed himself in the works of Ovid, particularly books 6 and 7 of the *Metamorphoses*. He wrote his Ovidian adaptations, the lost *Shoulder Bite* and the surviving *Philomena*. Vernacular adaptations of Latin classics appealed to noblewomen like Eleanor and Marie, who usually did not study Latin thoroughly enough to read it for pleasure. Henry II and Count Henri were well educated and read Latin literature easily.

When Count Henri returned to Troyes from the war, which ended in 1174, Chrétien may well have resumed the subject of King Arthur with *Cligès*. The Graeco-German setting of *Cligès* reflects the world of Count Henri of Champagne, who had traveled in the Byzantine Empire and the Holy Roman Empire. Count Henri had been in negotiations with Frederick Barbarossa in 1171 or 1172, representing Louis VII in a treaty to expel Brabantine mercenaries from German and French territories.[43] Between 1170 and 1174, Frederick Barbarossa was in political and marital negotiations with the Byzantine emperor Manuel Comnenus, which entailed a visit by a Greek ambassador to Cologne and involvement by Henry the Lion, duke of Saxony, in negotiations in Constantinople in 1172.[44] The titles and towns are echoed in *Cligès*. Count Henri was personally acquainted with both the German emperor and the Byzantine emperor.[45] Thus the setting of *Cligès* would have appealed to him as a literary patron because it reflected his travels and diplomatic experiences.[46]

This grouping of Chrétien's works by British and Ovidian themes is a more complicated approach to the chronology of his works. It is simpler to assume that his shorter works preceded his first long romance of *Erec*. Nonetheless such literary experimentation during an unsettled period is consistent with the stated purpose of *Guillaume*, the citation from Wace's *Rou* in *Philomena*,[47] the influence of Ovid's *Metamorphoses* on *Cligès*, and the major change in Chrétien's writing style that occurred during the hiatus between *Erec* and *Cligès*. This analysis argues that the works in the prologue to *Cligès* are approximately in chronological order, not reverse chronological order, so that the adaptations of Ovid were written between *Erec* and *Cligès*.

The realistic features of the romances of Chrétien de Troyes reflect the historical context in which the poet was writing. This historical and genealogical background does not explain every feature of the literary work, but it can be helpful in explaining some aspects. Troubadours and fairs were not the only channels of communication between England and France. Court visits by noblemen and clergy and their entourages contributed to the flow of literary and factual information. The count and countess of Champagne are often considered in isolation. Their extensive kinship network may have been an important contribution to the endeavors of their court poet, Chrétien de Troyes, and is reflected in *Cligès*.

SUMMARY

In the prologue Chrétien lists his works as *Erec and Enide*, the *Commandments* of Ovid and Ovid's *Art of Love* in French, *The Shoulder Bite*, *King Mark and Fair Isolde*, and a tale about "the metamorphosis of hoopoe, swallow, and nightingale." He also includes the source for his romance and the topos of the passage of culture from the ancient to the modern world.

Alexander, the elder son of the emperor of Constantinople, travels to King Arthur's court with an entourage to prepare for being knighted. King Arthur decides to travel to Brittany and entrusts England to Count Angrès of Windsor. Queen Guinevere sails accompanied by Sir Gawain's sister, a maiden named Soredamors, hitherto disdainful of love. Both Soredamors and Alexander are struck by Cupid's arrow, and their lovesickness catches the queen's attention, although she initially mistakes their emotion for motion sickness. Anguished love monologues ensue. After a pleasant summer in Brittany, King Arthur receives the news that he has been betrayed by Count Angrès, who has claimed his realm and amassed an army in London. King Arthur assembles an army and sails for England; Alexander asks and receives the king's permission to be knighted so that he may join the fight. The queen gives Alexander the gift of a chemise stitched with gold thread combined with the blond hair of Soredamors.

Count Angrès flees with his men from London to Windsor Castle, and King Arthur lays siege to the fortress. Alexander and his Greek companions capture four of Count Angrès's men on the banks of the Thames and present them to Queen Guinevere for safekeeping. King Arthur demands that the queen surrender the traitors to him, and he has them drawn by horses around Windsor Castle until their limbs lie scattered in the fields. King Arthur's initial assault on the cliff side of the castle fails, and the king offers a golden cup to the man who can penetrate the castle. The traitors take counsel and decide that their only hope lies in surprising the king's forces while they are asleep. Raiding parties leave the castle under cover of darkness. They are revealed by the moonlight on their shields and driven back to the castle. Alexander and a party penetrate the castle by donning the armor of dead traitors, seize the upper ward, and capture Count Angrès in the keep. The traitors surrender to King Arthur, and Alexander wins both the golden cup and the hand of Soredamors in marriage. Their son is named Cligès.

When Alexander's father dies, false news is given that Alexander has died at sea, and his younger brother Alis is crowned emperor of Constantinople. Alexander reaches a settlement with his brother whereby Alis retains the crown but vows not to marry, so that the succession will pass to his nephew Cligès. Subsequently Alexander dies, recommending that Cligès prove himself as a knight in Britain, and Soredamors dies of grief. After some years Alis breaks his vow and agrees to marry; his choice is Fenice, the daughter of the emperor of Germany. Since she has been promised to the duke of Saxony, Alis goes with fourteen-year-old Cligès and an army to fetch her in Cologne. Cligès and Fenice fall in love; the Saxon duke sends a warning via his nephew, who challenges Cligès to a tourney and is overthrown. Fenice, deeply troubled that she is being betrothed to the uncle although she loves the nephew and unwilling to become another Isolde, confides in her governess, Thessala of Thessaly. The governess brews a magic potion for Alis to consume on his wedding night that makes him sleep while giving him erotic dreams that he has taken possession of his wife.

At Regensburg Alis's party is challenged by the duke of Saxony, and Cligès slays the duke's nephew. Cligès dons the armor of the dead Saxon youth and lures the opposing forces into battle. Seeing the armies engaged, a spy suggests that the Saxon duke send a party to abduct the unguarded Fenice, but Cligès rescues her and returns her to his uncle. Cligès is challenged by the duke of Saxony to single combat. At Cligès's request, Alis dubs him a knight and gives him white arms for combat. Cligès is inspired by Fenice's outcry when he is nearly downed, and he defeats his formidable Saxon foe.

Cligès separates from Alis's party near Regensburg to travel to Britain, and Fenice mourns his absence. In Britain, Cligès fights in a great tournament in Wallingford, where, as an unknown knight, on three separate days, attired in three different sets of armor and mounted on three different horses, he defeats King Arthur's finest knights, Sagremore, Lancelot, and Perceval and then ties with Sir Gawain.

Lovesick, Cligès returns to Greece and Fenice, and they avow their love for one another. With Thessala's help they formulate a plan to be united. Fenice will feign illness, consume a potion brewed by Thessala that will make her seem dead, and be buried in a tomb. With the assistance of his serf John, Cligès will rescue her and spirit her away. John has already prepared the hiding place: the secret apartments of a sumptuous tower with hot running water. The plan is complicated by the arrival of three physicians, who find Fenice's pulse, flog her, and pour boiling lead through her palms in an attempt to force the "dead" woman to speak. The physicians are lynched by an angry mob of women, and Alis buries and mourns his inert wife. Fenice is released from her tomb and recovers from her injuries in the tower.

The lovers spend a rapturous year and three months in the tower, the latter part slumbering outdoors in a beautiful garden and orchard, where they are surprised by a knight named Bertrand. Although Cligès cuts off Bertrand's leg, the knight lives long enough to tell his tale to the emperor, and the lovers flee with Thessala to Britain. King Arthur assembles a fleet to sail to Constantinople to defend Cligès's rights, but the serf John arrives with the news that Alis has died and Cligès is the new emperor. Cligès and Fenice return to Greece and are married and crowned. While they live happily ever after, subsequent emperors of Constantinople, appalled by Fenice's example, resolve to keep their wives in seclusion, guarded by eunuchs.

CHRÉTIEN'S SOURCES

Cligès has multiple sources. It is a fusion of classical and medieval stories, Celtic legend, *chanson de geste*, and dubious history. *Cligès* is a two-part romance, like *Tristan*, telling first of the marriage and death of the hero's parents, Alexander and Soredamors, and then of the adventures of the hero himself. The first part of the romance, with its theme of a king betrayed by a trusted lord, in particular one acting as regent, is taken partly from the *Song of Roland*. Chrétien refers specifically to the traitor Ganelon, who betrays Charlemagne by arranging for his nephew Roland to be killed and is punished by being drawn apart by four horses.[48] *Cligès* also reflects the tale contained in Geoffrey of Monmouth's *History of the Kings of Britain* about King Arthur's betrayal by Mordred when the king has nearly reached Rome: Mordred bigamously marries Queen Guinevere and begins to rule Arthur's kingdom from London Tower. Its intricate love monologues are in the Ovidian tradition. The invasion of Windsor Castle seems to be based on direct observation of the fortress and its surroundings.

Chrétien claims to have found the tale on which the second part of the romance is based in the monastery library of St. Peter of Beauvais. Although he may be using the topos of a prestigious and imaginary source to enhance his credibility, there is no immediate reason to disbelieve him. A clergyman would have had access to such a library. This tale may have been a version of a story of an anonymous Grecian empress who commits adultery, without potions or a feigned death, with a nephew of her husband's named Cligès that was written down subsequently in the thirteenth-century compilation entitled *Marques de Rome*.[49] This tale may also be a version of an oriental story known as *Solomon's Wife* or *La Fausse Morte* in which a wife feigns death to escape an unwanted husband. Later it became the source for Shakespeare's *Romeo and Juliet*. Another source was the popular Tristan legend, which dominates *Cligès* and *Lancelot*. Chrétien seems to have been troubled by the popularity of the adulterous triangle between king, queen, and nephew. His *Cligès* has been termed an anti-*Tristan*, in which the characters, particularly the heroine, Fenice, react violently against the legend. Although the names of King Mark, Queen Isolde, Tristan, Morholt, and Brangien have been changed to Emperor Alis, Fenice, Cligès, the duke of Saxony, and Thessala, the characters in *Cligès* recall the Tristan legend, with the ruler deceived by his nephew and his wife with the help of her servant, who provides a magic potion, as well as a serf named John who provides a refuge for the lovers. The idyllic tower where the lovers meet invokes the "salle aux images" (hall of statues), one of numerous other references to Thomas's *Tristan* throughout the romance.

Together with the love monologues inspired by Ovid, Chrétien has also incorporated into the romance other references to tales of unhappy lovers that appear in the *Metamorphoses*. These tales are concentrated in book 6 and the beginning of book 7, which suggests that Chrétien was working with the Latin original. In connection with Fenice and Cligès he mentions the love affairs of Medea and Jason, Helen and Paris, Myrrha and Cintras, and Narcissus and Echo and evokes the tale of the suicides of Pyramus and Thisbe. None of these affairs is a particularly fortunate or inspirational model. Yet this fusion of literary sources marks a significant transition from *Erec* to Chrétien's mature works. In *Cligès*, Chrétien did not faithfully follow the plot structure of a Welsh *mabinogi*. He had developed the confidence to create a truly original work.

As *Erec and Enide* is the model for Chrétien's subsequent romance, *Yvain; or, The Knight with the Lion, Cligès* is the model for the romance written concurrently with *Yvain, Lancelot; or, The Knight of the Cart*. Many themes in *Cligès* are repeated in *Lancelot*. The unguarded and unresisting married heroine is abducted by a powerful lord, who wants her for himself. There is great rejoicing when the heroine is returned to her husband. The abductor challenges the rescuer to a duel; if the rescuer wins, the heroine may remain with her husband and his court. In the ensuing duel, the hero falters and then is inspired by the heroine's outcry to greater feats of prowess. The phrase "I am totally your own" is used to express the lovers' commitment to one another. At a great tournament, the hero fights in disguise and wins the day. A meeting between the hero and the heroine after a long absence occurs in the presence of her husband and the court. The heroine longs to kiss and embrace the hero but realizes that such a display of emotion would be folly. A tower is an important edifice in the story. After the heroine is believed to be dead, an angry speech is made in which Death is personified as a whore. In a reworking of the legend of Pyramus and Thisbe, the hero considers suicide if the heroine is dead but learns that she is alive before taking his own life. Crucifixion imagery is used in both romances. In *Cligès*, Fenice falls with outstretched arms in the shape of a cross after crying out, "Saint Mary!" when Cligès takes a heavy blow from the duke of Saxony. Later she is flagellated and tortured with stigmata-like holes in her palms, anointed with precious ointment, enshrouded, and entombed. Lancelot's rescue of the prisoners of Gorre is likened to the "Harrowing of Hell," where the rescuer of those in the land from which none return crosses the sword bridge with bloody hands and feet and is anointed with the balm of the Three Marys. These common themes suggest that *Cligès* is a fairly recent precursor of *Lancelot*.

The youthful heroes of this romance are modeled after the wily Tristan and his classical predecessor, Ulysses. Alexander and particularly Cligès combine undoubted prowess and valor with a marked amount of cunning and guile. Neither one hesitates to don the armor worn by dead men on the opposing side and change insignia in order to penetrate enemy lines in disguise, a practice not universally admired and mentioned only in this romance. Cligès's cutting off the leg of the unarmed and fleeing Bertrand, who surprised the couple in the tower garden while hawking, is not an inspirational episode. Alexander and Cligès present a sharp contrast with the straightforward, frank heroes Erec and Yvain, not to mention the naive Perceval, but they do not seem exceptionally duplicitous in the atmosphere of broken promises and lies that prevails at the Byzantine court. Fortunately, these heroes reserve their deceitfulness for the battlefield and are constant in love, although the heroines, who ponder whether their love is sincere, seem justified in raising the issue.

Chrétien de Troyes is particularly gifted at creating female characters, and one of his most lovable is the tongue-tied Soredamors, who engages in lengthy silent love monologues and interior debates about Alexander without daring even to utter his name and open a conversation. If it were not for the perceptiveness of Queen Guinevere, who realizes that the young persons are in love and capably arranges their wedding, they might yet be sitting side by side in her tent in silence. One of the most salient features of Chrétien's creation of the literary character of Queen Guinevere is that she presides over the weddings of Erec and Alexander and takes great pleasure in enabling romantic love thus to find its honorable culmination. Fenice evokes Ovid's Medea in her concern about Cligès's sincerity of affection. Ironically, her desire to avoid a bad reputation culminates in the confinement of subsequent empresses to prevent them from emulating her deception. Yet her love is deep, and her character is developed by means of striking Christian symbolism. Her name means "phoenix," a symbol of the resurrection, and she is scourged and bears the equivalent of stigmata when boiling oil is poured through her palms, followed by her anointing, entombment, and release to a new life.

In *Cligès* Chrétien tempers his opposition to adultery by developing the idea of obtaining the bride's consent to marriage. Unlike Erec, who unhesitatingly arranges his own marriage to Enide with her father, Alexander scrupulously emphasizes that he has not requested Soredamors's hand in marriage as his boon from King Arthur for obtaining the surrender of Windsor Castle. He explains that he has not discussed marriage with Soredamors and does not want her to be coerced into marrying him. Fenice's marriage is arranged between Emperor Alis and her father without her permission and against her wishes. Her need to reconcile her horror of adultery with her aversion to her future husband results in her requesting Thessala to prepare the first potion that preserves her virginity and the second brew that simulates her death.[50] Although Fenice's situation is not presented as nobly as Erec's rescue of Enide from her forced marriage to the abusive Count Oringle of Limors in the previous romance, Chrétien stresses the importance of consent to marriage by the woman involved. Like his ideal of love within marriage, the idea would have seemed novel to his contemporaries.

Cligès has many parallels with Shakespeare's *Romeo and Juliet,* with which it may share a common source in the aforementioned tale of *Solomon's Wife.* Cligès and Fenice are about fourteen or fifteen years old. Fenice is very dependent upon the advice of her governess, and Cligès, an orphan, relies on his serf John and his great-uncle King Arthur. The young couple steadfastly resist the authority of older adults. Emperor Alis and the duke of Saxony intend to force Fenice to marry against her will. The duke seeks to kill Cligès, and Alis seeks to disinherit him. The idealism of their youthful passion induces the young couple to reject the adulterous compromise of Tristan and Isolde. It also induces them to take great risks with little fear of death. Cligès successfully challenges the best knights of Arthur's court. Fenice drinks a paralyzing potion and is nearly killed when the physicians subject her to unforeseen tortures. After their year of passion in the seclusion of the tower and orchard, their irregular situation is resolved by a lawful marriage and a dual coronation. Like *Erec,* the romance ends when the lovers assume their public roles in society. Chrétien will draw on his portraits of the youthful Fenice and Cligès when he creates his masterpiece *Perceval.*

Chrétien portrays the aristocracy and devotes little space or sympathy to the motivations of the peasant or merchant classes in his romances. For this reason, his portrait of Cligès's loyal serf John, a skilled artisan and craftsman, is particularly interesting. Chrétien presents John as a man who is respected and well treated and who is engaged in a lucrative and independent trade. Yet John is not an agricultural serf tied to the land who owes his lord dues and several days a week of work or an artisan serf who owes his lord a portion of his earnings from his trade. John's serfdom is a form of slavery, and his status resembles that of a Greek urban slave whose life and possessions are at his owner's mercy. Chrétien emphasizes John's longing for freedom for himself and his family. Later he portrays John as prepared to die in order to protect Cligès and Fenice and to confront Emperor Alis bluntly about his broken promise. When Cligès is told that he is the new emperor of Constantinople, he knows the news is true because of John's well-known reputation for honesty and accuracy. Nowhere else does Chrétien portray a commoner so sympathetically. John is an eloquent argument for the abolition of slavery, which persisted in the twelfth century along the Mediterranean shores.[51]

THE MANUSCRIPT TRADITION

Cligès is preserved in the following manuscripts:

Florence, Ricc. 2756, excerpt
Oxford, Bodl., Michael 569 (SC 24064), fragments
Paris, BN, fr. 375 (P)
Paris, BN, fr. 794 (A)
Paris, BN, fr. 1374 (S)
Paris, BN, fr. 1420 (R)
Paris, BN, fr. 1450 (B)
Paris, BN, fr. 12560 (C)
Tours, BM 942 (M)
Turin, BNU L. I. 13 (1626) (T)
Private collection, Annonay fragments[52]

This translation is based on BN, fr. 794, known as the Guiot copy, which was edited by Alexandre Micha and published in the series of Les classiques français du moyen âge. BN, fr. 794, contains a reference to an incident in which the Greek emperor sees a severed head on Cligès's lance tip and mistakes it for Cligès's head (vv. 3491–3492) that is not contained in other manuscripts. There is also a specific reference to Tristan and Isolde that is omitted in three manuscripts (vv. 5199–5202). The translation contains some minor couplets and proverbs that are omitted in BN, fr. 794, but are included in most other manuscripts, as well as a description of the dead lying along the Thames riverbank (vv. 2100ff.); Alexander giving the golden cup he won to Sir Gawain (vv. 2199ff.); Cligès telling his name to the one Saxon he spares to carry the news of their defeat to the duke (vv. 3770ff.); an expansion on Fenice's assurances to Cligès that she would be happier with him in humble surroundings than in a palace (vv. 5296ff.); an expansion on the importance Cligès attaches to discretion in his arrangements with John (vv. 5464ff.); false assurances of loyalty made by the physicians to the inert Fenice (vv. 5872ff.); an elaboration on the mutual bliss found by Fenice and Cligès in the tower (vv. 6258ff.); and a lengthy affirmation by John of his loyalty to his master Cligès and his disapproval of the emperor's breaking of his promise not to marry (vv. 6462ff.). These variants and interpolations are indicated by letters, so that the numbering of the verses of the translation corresponds to the numbering of BN, fr. 794.

TRANSLATOR'S NOTE

I have long argued that form is as intrinsic a part of a literary work as substance. Rhyme and meter establish the pace of Chrétien's romances and accommodate his wordplay. The benefits of verse translation are most evident in *Cligès*. In his preceding romance, *Erec*, Chrétien prepares long lists of names and develops the technique of the lengthy description. Both these lists and these descriptions are cleverer and faster paced in verse translation. In *Cligès*, Chrétien develops the technique of the monologue, particularly the love monologue. These monologues replace tears and allow the characters to explore their deepest feelings. They sparkle with witty play on key words and ponder such issues as how two hearts can be one and offer different explanations. They show the preoccupation of young persons in love with the subtle meanings of commonplace expressions, conversational openings, or even a strand of hair. They are intricate introspective monologues and show considerable sophistication in substance as well as rhetorical skill. Nonetheless, they would seem interminable if they were not punctuated by rhyme and accelerated by meter. The case for verse translation rests on the difference between a sonnet and a paragraph, and it is best illustrated in this early romance.

Cligès is the least known of Chrétien's romances. It is unfairly considered to be an atypical Arthurian romance because of the Byzantine setting of the second part. In its two-part structure it lacks the unity of *Lancelot* and *Yvain*. Like the lengthy descriptions in his earliest romance, *Erec and Enide*, the love monologues in *Cligès* are decidedly overdone. Notwithstanding, *Cligès* is an important transitional work. It represents a more sensitive development of courtly love. It introduces the love monologues, word play, topoi and influence of Ovid that brighten the later works. It is Chrétien's first adaptation of the Tristan legend and contains the seeds of his second adaptation of the legend, his masterpiece *Lancelot*. Its heroines are fine additions to his perceptive portraits of women and reflect his consistent concern with the issue of consensual marital relations. It is unique in its depiction of slavery. It is brought to a satisfactory conclusion. *Cligès* merits much more attention than it has received, for it foreshadows the genius and style of Chrétien's later and more popular romances.

CLIGÈS

PROLOGUE

HE who wrote *Erec and Enide,*
    Commandments Ovid once decreed
and *Art of Love* in French did write,
and wrote about the shoulder bite,
about King Mark and fair Isolde,
the metamorphosis retold
of hoopoe, swallow, nightingale,*
about a youth begins a tale
who was in Greece, kin to King Arthur.
But you shall hear about his father　　　　　　10
before I tell you of the lad:
from where he came, what life he had,
what lineage had been his part.
His father, brave and bold of heart,
to conquer honor and acclaim,
left Greece and on to England came,
which at that time was known as Britain,
and we can find this story written
in one book of the tomes contained
within the library maintained　　　　　　　　20
at Lord St. Peter of Beauvais.*
The tale was taken from that place　　　　　　22
for this romance Chrétien has done.　　　　　　a
The volume is an ancient one　　　　　　　　　b
that has this true tale, where I read it,　　　　23
which makes it worthier of credit.
Through books we own we have been taught
about the deeds the ancients wrought
and life and times in days of old.
Our books taught us Greece was extolled

[1]

both first and most prestigiously
30 for learning and for chivalry.
Then chivalry came next to Rome;
now all that knowledge has come home
to France, where, if God has ordained,
God grant that it may be retained.
God grant the region so enchants
the honor that has paused in France
that nevermore from France be flown
what God gave others as a loan.
For nowadays no person speaks
40 about the Romans or the Greeks;
no further words of them are said;
their glowing coals are quenched and dead.*

KING ARTHUR'S COURT

SO Chretien initiates
his story as the book relates,
and it concerns an emperor
with wealth and honor in great store
who ruled Greece and Constantinople.
His empress, elegant and noble,
bore him two sons as progeny.
50 The firstborn reached maturity
before the other's date of birth
and could, if he had seen the worth,
be knighted and assume control
and rule the empire as a whole,
and Alexander was that child;
the younger as Alis was styled.
Their sire bore Alexander's name;
their mother Tantalis could claim.
About the Empress Tantalis,

[2]

about the emperor and Alis   60
we shall make no more mention here;
of Alexander you shall hear.*
The pride and courage he displayed
were such that any accolade
in his own region he disdained.
About King Arthur, who then reigned,
he had heard mention and report,
and of the barons at his court,
who made it feared and well renowned
throughout the whole wide world around   70
and kept him constant company.
Whatever outcome might there be
or incident might be incurred,
still Alexander, undeterred,
sought Britain. Yet he must receive
his father's leave and take his leave
before the young man could be bound
to Britain and to Cornwall's bound.
To take and seek his leave before,
he went to see the emperor.   80
So Alexander, brave and fair,
would tell his wishes and declare
what he would venture and essay.
"Dear father, to learn honor's way,
to win esteem and fame to savor,
I dare to ask you for a favor
that I would have you grant to me.
If you are willing to agree,
do not delay but be direct."
The emperor did not expect   90
to be distressed by what he gave.
He did most covet and most crave
high honor for his elder son
and thought the boon would be well done.

[3]

Thought? Would be, were he to augment
that honor by his full consent.
"Dear son, your pleasure I shall grant,
and you must tell me what you want,
for I shall grant you what you ask."
100   The youth had well performed his task,
and he was very pleased indeed
the boon was granted and agreed
that he had been desiring so.
"This boon, sire, would you like to know?"
he said. "I want a manifold
sum of your silver and your gold;
I want companions from your train,
as many as I shall ordain,
because I now intend to quit
110   your empire, and the benefit
of my own services I'll bring
and offer Britain's ruling king,
so that he may make me a knight.
I pledge my word to you outright:
I have resolved I'll never lace
my helm on head or arm my face
on any day I live until
King Arthur, if he deigns and will,
and no one else, clasps on my sword."*
120   A thought the emperor deplored:
"Good Lord, dear son, don't take that tone!
This land has just become your own,
and rich Constantinople, plus.
Do not think me penurious;
what I shall give you is renowned.
Tomorrow I shall have you crowned;
tomorrow too you shall be knighted.
Then you shall rule all Greece united,
and barons shall accord to you

[4]

the oaths and homage you are due,   130
which pledges they must solemnize.
Refusing this would be unwise."
The young man heard his father say
he'd dub him knight past mass next day,
a promise of which he was sure,
yet said he would prove good or poor
in some land other than his own.
"If what I seek you will condone,
with what I asked you to confer,
then give me vair and grayish fur,   140
good horses, cloth of silken stuff.
My fighting skills are not enough
for me to carry arms by right.
Before I have become a knight,
King Arthur is the one I'd serve.
No prayers or flattery can swerve
the resolution I have planned
to travel to the foreign land
where this king and his lords are found,
who are exceedingly renowned   150
for courtesy and excellence.
So many lords, through indolence,
forego the praise they would be worth
if they had traveled through the earth.
Repose and excellent repute,
in my opinion, poorly suit.
A rich man set in idle ways
acquires no reason for self-praise.   158
So valor weighs upon the knave   a
as cowardice upon the brave.   b
Acclaim and rest do not accord.   159
So any man whose sole reward   160
is gaining wealth without digressions
becomes a slave to his possessions.

[5]

Dear father, if I merit fame,
as long as I can seek acclaim,
I shall endeavor to do so."
The emperor felt joy and woe
about this matter, that is clear.
The emperor felt joy to hear
his son sought fame and woebegone
170   because the young man would be gone;
but he had granted him the boon,
though it might prove inopportune,
and was committed to comply.
No emperor should tell a lie.
"Dear son, since you are so intent
on honor and accomplishment,
I must not fail to do your pleasure;
with gold and silver from my treasure
you can load up two barges full,
180   but in largess be bountiful."
The youth was courteous, well bred,
and joyous that his father said
that he would further his proposal,
and place his wealth at his disposal,
and gave him counsel and command
to give and spend with open hand,
and told him why to do no less.
"My dear son, I believe largess
to be a lady and a queen
190   who gives all virtues light and sheen.
The proof is easy to discern:
to what good works can someone turn,
though wealth and power he may keep,
and not be shamed if he is cheap?
His other virtues seem the less
without some praise for his largess.
Largess creates, by its own worth,

[6]

a gentleman, not noble birth,
not courteous manners, not discretion,
not great refinement, not possession,   200
not strength, not knightly chivalry,
not prowess, not authority,
not good looks, nor another trait.
The rose's beauty is more great
than any flower that ever grew
when first it opens, fresh and new,
so where largess's gifts are cast,
all other virtues are surpassed;
those qualities it may unearth
in gentlemen of proven worth   210
largess expands five-hundredfold.
So much about it can be told
I could not say the half of it."
The young man got him to commit
all he might seek and might desire,
so that, on orders from his sire,
whatever he desired he had.
The empress felt extremely sad
when she heard tell and came to know
the way her son was bound to go,   220
and yet, no matter who felt riled
or thought he acted like a child
or warned against it or demurred,
the young man instantly sent word
to fit his ships out and prepare,
because the young man did not care
to tarry in his native land.
So, at his order and command,
that night they loaded up his fleet
with hard tack and with wine and meat.   230
At port the ships were stocked with store.
The following morning, to the shore

came Alexander, quite transported,
by his companions well escorted.
The voyage made them pleased and glad.
The empress, who was very sad,
and emperor came with them too.
At port beside the cliff, the crew
of sailors in the ships were seen;
240 the weather peaceful and serene;
the air was clear, the wind dispersed.
Then Alexander was the first
when from his father he had parted
and took his mother's leave (sorehearted,
her heart ached in her chest and throat)
to board the vessel from a boat,
and his companions boarded too,
together, four and three and two,
in haste to board ship undelayed.
250 The sail was raised, the anchor weighed.
Immediately the vessels left.
The ones at home, who felt bereft
to see the young man on his route,
allowed their eyes to give pursuit
while there were outlines to pursue.
So they could have a better view
and watch him for a longer time,
together they began to climb
a hill, and from that high relief
260 they gazed upon their cause of grief.
While they could see their friend, with care
they watched in sorrow and despair
about the young man leaving court
and prayed God lead him safe to port
without misfortune or great peril.
They were at sea the month of April
entirely and a part of May.

[8]

Without great peril or dismay
below Southampton town they dropped
their anchor at a port and stopped   270
between none and the vesper hour.
The youths, who'd not acquired the power
to cope with misery and pain,
had been obliged long to remain
upon the sea till all were pale
from seasickness and weak and frail,
including those whose health was best,
the strongest and the hardiest.
Yet they rejoiced exceedingly
when once they had escaped the sea   280
and had arrived where they thought right.
Below Southampton, overnight
they celebrated and reposed
because they were so indisposed,
inquiring if the king were found
within the realm of England's bound.
He was at Winchester, they learned,
and if, when daybreak was discerned,
they rose and took the straight way down,
in quite good time they'd reach the town.   290
This news was pleasing to the ear.   a
The morrow, as the dawn came near,   b
at early morn the youths arose   291
and donned accoutrement and clothes,
and once the youths were well arrayed,
they left Southampton, and they stayed
unswerving on the straight main road
until they reached the king's abode;
it was at Winchester that time.
Before the hour had come for prime,
the Greeks arrived, their journey short,
dismounting at the stairs to court.   300

[9]

The squires and horses in their care
stayed in the courtyard. Up the stair
the young men climbed to where they found
the finest king the world around
who ever was or is to be.
When he observed their company,
King Arthur felt glad and content.
The company, before they went
before the king, removed their cloaks
310   lest they be reckoned simple folks.
Thus, mantles all abandoning,
the youths appeared before the king.
The lords all met them with a stare
and thought them nobly born and fair,
because the youths seemed very pleasant.
They did not doubt the young men present
were all the sons of kings and counts,
and that was true on all accounts.
The youths were at a handsome age,
320   well built, of noble lineage,
and long of limb, with garments made
identical in cut and shade,
all from one fabric, in accord.
They numbered twelve without their lord.
I'll say that much of him, no more,
no one born was superior.
Thus, unpretentious, unplumed,
well built and handsome and well groomed,
uncloaked, the young lord came to meet
330   the king and knelt down at his feet;
the others all with one accord
knelt from affection by their lord.
Then Alexander, smooth of tongue,
whence eloquence and wisdom sprung,
addressed King Arthur, whom he hailed.

"Oh, king, unless untruths prevailed
when your fame was by Fame portrayed,
since the first man God ever made
no king with faith in God on earth
as powerful has come to birth.　　　　　　　　340
Oh, king, your fame of wide report
is what has brought me to your court,
so I can serve and honor you
and stay here in your retinue
until I am a new-made knight
(and if you find my service right)
by your hand, not another's, made.
If you won't give my accolade,
I shan't be called a knight unless
I please you with my services.　　　　　　　　350
If they would cause you such delight,
good king, that you'll make me a knight,
let me and my companions bide."
　　The king immediately replied:
"My friend, I certainly agree
to keep you and your company,
and all of you are welcome here,
for I believe that it seems clear
you're sons of men who are well bred.
From where are you?" "From Greece," they said.　360
"From Greece?" "True." "What's your father's rank?"
"The emperor, sire, to be frank."
"My dear friend, what name do you claim?"
"They gave me Alexander's name
where I received the salt and chrism
and Christian faith at my baptism."
"So, Alexander, cherished friend,
you did me honor to attend
my court, and gladly hitherto
I'll keep you in my retinue.　　　　　　　　370

[11]

It makes me greatly pleased and cheered.
I want to have you be revered,
as noble, wise, and quick to please.
You've been too long upon your knees.
Now I direct you all to stand
and from this day at my command
be of my intimates and court.
You have arrived at a good port."
Upon these words the Greeks arose,
380   pleased that the king so nobly chose
and Alexander was retained.
At court he was well entertained.
Whatever he sought, there was no dearth,
and every lord, though high of birth,
was welcoming to him and charming.
No youth was nobler, more disarming,
and of conceit he had no stain.
He came to know the lord Gawain
and other courtiers one by one,
390   becoming loved by everyone.
Such love did Sir Gawain extend,
he called the youth "companion," "friend."
The Greeks went where a burgher dwelt
and took town lodgings that they felt
the best place they could have to board.
Now Alexander brought a hoard
of wealth with him from Constantinople,
and, as the emperor thought noble
and counseled him when they did part
400   and bade him to have an open heart
in spending liberally and giving,
largess became his way of living.
His efforts thereto were heartfelt.
He lived well at the place he dwelt,
and, as his riches authorized

[12]

and his heart counseled and advised,
he generously gave and spent.
The court was lost in wonderment
at where he found these vast amounts.
To everyone he gave fine mounts   410
from his own land that he had brought.
By good deeds Alexander sought
and served so well and strove so hard
he won the king's love and regard
and that of all his lords and queen.

LOVE LAMENTS

KING ARTHUR, at that time, was keen
to travel into Brittany.
He called his barons in to see
what person he should designate
as regent of the English state,   420
to guard and keep his land at peace
until his traveling should cease.
The lords in council thought it just,
in my view, for him to entrust
the realm to Windsor's Count Angrès.
A lord of more trustworthiness,
they counseled him, could not be found
within the realm throughout its bound.
King Arthur, once he placed his land
with Count Angrès and in his hand,   430
moved queen and maids the following day.
The king and lords were on their way.
In Brittany this news was voiced;
the Bretons mightily rejoiced.
No youth or maiden on the trip
was crossing on the monarch's ship

but Alexander, he alone.
The queen, indeed it should be known,
brought Soredamors upon the main,
440   one who held love in great disdain.*
No one had ever heard tell of
a man whom she would deign to love,
whatever his good looks, his worth,
authority, or noble birth.
The maiden, though she was unfeeling,
was beautiful and so appealing
she should have learned of Love indeed,
had she been pleased to pay him heed,
but never paid him any mind.
450   It made the God of Love inclined
to make her sorry for her distance
and be avenged for the resistance
and haughtiness she felt his due.*
Love aimed his arrow, straight and true,
and through the heart she was impaled
and often sweat and often paled.
She loved in spite of her disdain;
it took great effort to refrain
from looking Alexander's way.
460   How dearly she must buy and pay
for her great pride and disregard,
and yet she must be on her guard
against her brother, Sir Gawain.
Love heated her a bath of pain,
and one she found extremely hot.
Now it felt good, now it did not,
now she desired it, now refused;
her eyes of treason she accused*
and said: "You have betrayed me, eyes,
470   for you have made my heart despise
and hate me, though once true to me.

[14]

I am distressed by what I see.
Distressed? Why, no, I acquiesce.
If something I see means distress,
can I not keep my eyes controlled?
For I believe my strength would fold
and I would pay myself no mind,
could I not keep my eyes confined
by turning elsewhere my regard.
So thus I can be on my guard   480
against Love, who would master me.
Heart cannot mourn what eyes don't see.
If I see nought, it will mean nought,
and nought of me has he besought.   484
He would have sought me if he loved.   a
Since I'm not cherished or beloved,   b
will I love him if he's unfeeling?   485
Well, if my eyes find him appealing
when his good looks my eyes reveal
and they respond to his appeal,
should I say I love him thereby?
I should not; it would be a lie.   490
No claim to me can he profess,
nor claim against me, more or less.
One cannot love with eyes alone.
What wrong toward me have my eyes shown
for looking at what I see fit?
What fault or wrong did they commit?
Ought I to blame my eyes or chide them?
No! Blame whom then? Myself; I guide them.
My eyes don't look on any parts
that aren't the pleasure of my heart's.   500
My heart ought not to will a thing
that hurts; its will brings suffering.
I suffer? Then I am a fool:
I foolishly will what is cruel,

[15]

a will that I should overcome,
if I can, when it's troublesome.
If I can? Fool, what rigmarole!
For if I have no self-control,
what I can do will not be great.

510   Does Love think he can put me straight
when he leads others roundabout?
The others he may straighten out.
I am not his, nor was so painted,
nor will be, nor would be acquainted."
Thus go her personal debates.
Sometimes she loves, sometimes she hates,
so insecure she does not know
which way would be the best to go.
Although she thinks she can prevail,

520   defense from Love's of no avail.
Moreover, Heavens! In all candor
she does not know that Alexander
is holding her in constant thought.
So Love divides what he has brought
by giving each an equal share.
Love is impartial with the pair:
They love each other; they both yearn.
Had each been able to discern
the other's will and point of view,

530   it would be loyal love and true,
but what she wills he can't foretell,
nor does she know why he's unwell.
Their state was noted by the queen.
One and another she had seen
repeatedly turn pale and gray,
but when they acted in that way,
she did not know why it should be,
except because they were at sea.
Her grasp might have been more complete,

[16]

were it not for the sea's deceit.   540
The sea deceived her by its motion.
At sea she did not see emotion.
They came to love; they were at sea;
from love came rue the two do see;*
and of these three, the queen could name
none other than the sea to blame.
The third one was by two accused;
and by the third two felt excused,
when they were guilty all along.
Yet oft by one who did no wrong   550
another's sins are expiated.
The queen thus strongly inculpated
the sea and held it much to blame,
wherein she wrongly laid the blame.
The fault did not lie with the sea.
Soredamors in misery
remained until the ship reached port.
The king arrived to wide report.
The Bretons viewed him with delight,
and as their own liege lord by right   560
they served the king without reserve.
There is no more I shall observe
about King Arthur here and now,
so you will hear me tell you how
Love caused two lovers torments cruel
with whom he undertook to duel.
Thus Alexander, enamored of
the girl who sighed to have his love,
knew none of it and would not know
till for her sake he suffered woe   570
and pain that were excruciating.
He served the queen and maids in waiting,
because Love made him so inclined,
but to the one most on his mind

[17]

he did not speak a word outright.
If she had dared assert the right
to him she felt to be her own,
he would have made his feelings known,
but she ought not and did not dare.
580   It was distressing to the pair
to see each other in this way
with no more they could do or say.
Their love ignited and increased.
All lovers willingly will feast
their eyes, their glances they unfetter,
if they cannot do any better,
and they believe, because looks suit
that make love grow on taking root,
their gazes should help their desire.
590   Their gazes harm; one who nears fire
sustains a burn far more severe
than one who backs off and keeps clear.
Although their love more strongly flashed,
each made the other one abashed.
The pair were careful to conceal
and cover up what each might feel,
so there appeared no smoke or flash*
of flame from coals beneath the ash,
and yet the heat was not less strong,
600   because heat lingers far more long
beneath the ashes than above.
Both were in anguish from their love.
So their complaint stayed unperceived.
Each of necessity deceived
all people by a false pretense,
and yet each one raised loud laments
in privacy when evening fell.
Of Alexander first I'll tell,
how he lamented and complained.

[18]

The one for whom he felt so pained,   610
the one who stole away his heart,
Love pictured as a work of art.
Within his bed his rest was spare;
her loveliness and gracious air
he was well pleased to recollect
without a hope he could expect
that good results for him would rule.
"A fool, I think myself a fool.*
A fool? I am a fool to shrink
from speaking of the things I think,   620
for it would cause me more distress.
My thinking's turned to foolishness.
Far better I think like a fool
than, as a fool, take ridicule.
Will ever what I will be known?
Shall I conceal pain I bemoan
and never know how to obtain
both help and succor for my pain?
A fool is he who does not seek
good health and help when ill and weak,   630
if he can find them any place.
But many people think they chase
their own self-interest and relief;
instead they purchase pain and grief.
Who would seek someone to consult
who thinks good health would not result?
It would be laboring in vain.
My ill's so serious in vein,
I'll have no cure of origin
in any brew or medicine   640
or herb or root I may procure.
Not every illness has a cure.
The roots of mine are so deep set
No cure or treatment can I get.

Can't get? I lied. Had I disclosed
this illness when first indisposed,
dared tell of my indisposition,
I could have talked with the physician
who could have rendered full assistance.
650   It hurts to talk of its existence;
the doctor might not condescend
to take a fee or to attend.
A wonder, yet it brings me woe:
I'm very ill, and I don't know
what illness is tormenting me
and causing pain and agony.
Don't know? Oh yes, I think I know.
Love caused these ills I undergo.
But how? Can Love be ill inclined?
660   Is not Love gracious, good, and kind?
I thought in Love there could be shown
nothing but good and good alone
but find him wicked in his ways.
Nobody knows what game Love plays
until he enters in the fun.
Fool he who plays with such a one;
to harm his own is Love's sole care.
Indeed, his game is most unfair;
it's dangerous to play Love's game;
670   I think my downfall is his aim.
What shall I do? Should I withdraw?
Withdrawal seems to have no flaw;
but how can I get out of reach?
If Love chastises me to teach,
with threats to make me learn the faster,
am I supposed to scorn my master?
Who scorns his master is a fool.
What Love would teach me in his school
I should absorb and should retain.

[20]

I may have very much to gain.   680
I am alarmed he beats me so.
With no plain sight of wound or blow,
yet I complain? Have I mistook?
Not with the injury I took:
his arrow struck me to the heart,
but he has not withdrawn his dart.*
Could blow to body be applied
and have no wound appear outside?
I want to know, you must reply!
How did he strike you? Through my eye.   690
Your eye? Did not he put it out?
No harm to eye to speak about,
but he has pained me to the heart.
The reason why you must impart,
how through the eye the arrow rushed
and left the eye unhurt, uncrushed.
If through the eye the arrow pressed,
why is there heart pain in the chest,
a pain the eye won't undergo
from taking the initial blow?   700
I can explain: the eye won't try
to understand the reason why
and could not do so from the start
but is the mirror of the heart,
a mirror through which feelings pass,
not wounding and not crushing glass,
the feelings that the heart expressed.
The heart is placed within the chest
the way a lighted candle's placed
within a lantern and encased.   710
Now, once the candle has departed,
no light will shine or be imparted,
but while the candle shall endure,
the lantern will not be obscure.

[21]

The flame can shine therein and manage
to do no injury or damage.
To window glass this truth pertains.
However strong and thick the panes,
the sunbeams leave the glass intact;
720   rays pass through panes that are not cracked.
Though strong and clear the glass may seem,
one sees more when a shining beam
has struck it than by glass alone.
The same applies, it should be known,
to lantern, eyes, and looking glass,
for through the eye the light does pass
by which the heart itself can see,
outside the body, what there be,
and many different things it views:
730   Some green, and others violet hues,
some blue, another scarlet flame.
Some it may praise, another blame,
some loathe, another much esteem,
but something mirrored that may seem
quite lovely when the heart perceives it,
if heart is not on guard, deceives it.
They have deceived myself and mine.
A mirrored ray my heart saw shine,
a ray that's caused me much chagrin
740   within the mirror lodged therein,
so my heart failed me in the end.
I am mistreated by my friend,
who overlooks me for my foe.
His treatment of me is so low,
I can charge him with felony.
I thought I had as friends these three:
my heart and my two eyes combined.
Instead they hate me, so I find.
Oh, Heavens! What friends shall I know,

when these three have become my foe,   750
a part of me whom they are killing?
My servants* think me overwilling.
They do all that their wills inspire,
not as I will and I desire.
Now truly I have learned and known
from those who robbed me of my own:
the love felt by a good lord ends
for a bad servant he befriends.
He will inevitably complain,
with a bad servant in his train,   760
whatever happens, soon or late.
What arrow,* I shall now relate,
was ordered for me and conveyed,
and how this dart is shaped and made.
With fear of failure I am fraught;
the arrow is so richly wrought,
it is no wonder if I fail,
when its appearance I detail,
yet I'll exert all my endeavor.
The feathers and the nock together   770
are set so close there is a trace
of separation and a space
like a hair parting, fine and narrow,
whereas the nock of this fair arrow
is straight and polished to a shine
with nothing further to refine.
The arrow's feathers have a tint
as if they all had gilding's glint,
however there is no gold leaf;
the feathers, in my firm belief,   780
shine with more sheen than gilt possesses.
The feathers are the golden tresses
I saw that day upon the ocean;
this arrow causes my devotion.

[23]

Lord! What a precious thing is mine!
And who with such a treasure mine
throughout his life would seek to hold
or covet other wealth or gold?
For I could swear for my own part
790   I'd long for nothing but this dart;
the feathers only and the nock
I would not trade for Antioch.
With two things I so highly praise,
how could one possibly appraise
what would be the remainder's price?
It is so lovely and so nice,
so good and meritorious
that I am very envious
to have again within my sight
800   the forehead that God made so bright,
a gleam no topaz could surpass,
or emerald, or looking glass.
All that is meaningless to know
for one who sees her eyes aglow;
to all toward whom her eyes may turn,
they seem like candles, two, aburn.
Whose speech could so delight the ears
to tell just how her face appears,
the shining face and straight fine nose?
810   There lily is eclipsed by rose,
and rose the lily does efface
and so illuminates her face.
What of the mouth, so small and smiling,
which God made knowingly beguiling
so all who saw it and observed
would think she smiled because it curved?
The teeth with which her mouth is graced?
They touch and are so tightly spaced
that they seem melded close together.

[24]

And Nature made a small endeavor 820
whereby more beauty was imparted.
Whoever saw her with lips parted
could only say her teeth must be
of silver or of ivory.
So full a record should be made
of everything to be portrayed
about the ears, the chin thereunder,
omissions would be no great wonder.
As for her throat, I say aloud
beside it crystal turns to cloud. 830
Her body is four times more white;
by ivory her hair seems light.
At broach and neckband I discovered
a patch of skin that was uncovered
and whiter than new-fallen snow.
I would have felt my pain and woe
alleviated in much part
if I had wholly viewed the dart.*
If I knew it, I'd use my craft
for a description of the shaft. 840
However, if I cannot give
descriptions or a narrative
of something I have not been shown,
it is through no fault of my own.
Love showed me nothing altogether
excepting for the nock and feather;
The arrow he concealed to tease:
the overdress and the chemise
worn by the maiden was its quiver.
That illness is what makes me shiver. 850
That is the dart, that is the ray
by which to churlish rage I stray.
I'm churlish to be raging so.
The firm commitment that I owe

[25]

to Love will not be broke or marred
because I flouted him or warred.
Let him treat me as he may use
his own, however he may choose,
for I so will it and so please;
860   I won't be rid of this disease.
I'd rather frequently succumb
than be restored to health that's come
from any source except the same
from where the pain and illness came."
Thus Alexander's strong complaint.
The maid's lament was not more faint;
she made as much lament, not less.
All night she was in such distress
she neither rested nor reposed.
870   Within her heart Love had enclosed
such fury and ambivalence
that her heart trouble was intense,
and she was anguished and distraught.
She wept the night through, overwrought,
and tossed and turned and cried and wailed;
in faintness her heart nearly failed.
The maid, when she had wept and anguished
and tossed and turned, gasped, sighed, and languished,
looked into her own heart to find
880   who was the man, and of what kind,
on whose account it was she bore
the torture that Love had in store.
But when she felt much less distraught
because she had a pleasant thought,
she turned and stretched out and perceived
that she was foolish and deceived
in all that she had thought of late.
The maid began a new debate*
by saying: "Fool, why should I care

if this youth's gracious in his air,   890
brave, generous, with courtly ways?
All to his honor and his praise.
What if he's fair of face and limb?
His good looks can go off with him!
They will, although I disapprove,
and none of them will I remove.
Remove? I will not have that done.
Were he as wise as Solomon,
with handsomeness by Nature graced
such that none greater could be placed   900
within a human man's physique,
and God gave my hands power to wreak
such havoc that it was destroyed,
I would not have him thus annoyed.
Could I, I'd make him with good will
much handsomer and wiser still.
I do not hate him, I contend,
but does that mean I am his friend?
No more than of another man.
Why think more of him, if he can   910
please me no better than another?
I don't know, I can do no other,
for never have my thoughts so whirled
round any man in all the world.
I want to see him night and day
and never take my eyes away,
he is so pleasing to my eyes.
Now, is this Love? Yes, I surmise.
He's in my thoughts, one and another;
I love him more than any other.   920
Now, I love him. Now, that's agreed.
I'll do my will, a grave misdeed,
provided he is not displeased.
But Love has me completely seized,

[27]

so I am foolish, stunned, and crazed,
with no defense that can be raised,
and forced to suffer his assault.
I've guarded myself to a fault
against him long, without defeat,
930   and never would be indiscreet
or do one thing he had in mind.
Now I am gracious, overkind.
Why should Love show me gratitude
when by love he has not accrued
a boon or service I provide?
Now Love has overpowered pride.
I'm at his pleasure, my will vaster
to love now that I have a master.
Now Love will teach me—I'll be taught?—
940   how I should serve him as I ought.
I'm well instructed in that wise.
In serving him I have been wise;
there was no blame for me to earn,
and I have nothing more to learn.
Love wants me, and I also want,
to be wise and not arrogant
but gracious and a friend to all,
all for one individual.
Should I love all because of one?
950   I should be nice to everyone.
Love does not teach or recommend
I be to all a loyal friend.
Love teaches what is good alone,
and not for nothing am I known
as Soredamors by name, whereof
I must be loved and I must love.
As through my name the proof I'll claim,
for I find love within my name.
Its first part, *sore*, since days of old,

has meant the color blond or gold. 960
The best gold is the shiniest,
and so I think my name the best,
for it contains the very shade
of gold that is the finest made.
Then, by *amors*, the ending of
my name, I think of perfect love,
for he who uses my real name
renews his love for me the same
as it was ever from the start,
and one half gilds the other part 970
with shining gilding laid above,
and Soredamors means "gilt with love."
No golden gilding is as fine
as is the gilt with which I shine.
Thus Love has greatly honored me
by gilding me so personally,
and, firm in purpose and belief,
I'll be his gilding of gold leaf
without complaining of it, ever.
I love now and shall love forever. 980
Whom? What an answer to demand!
The one I love at Love's command;
to no one else will my love go.
Who cares, when he will never know
unless I tell him that is true?
Unless I ask, what shall I do?
She who has something she desires
ought to request what she requires.
What? Should I tell him my request?
No. Why? No woman has transgressed 990
so far with such a wrongful plan
as to request love of a man
unless she'd wholly lost her mind.
I'd be a fool, the proven kind,

[29]

if from my mouth I'd ever broach
what would redound to my reproach.
When from my mouth he was apprised,
I think that I would be despised.
He'd take me frequently to task
1000   for having been the first to ask.
May Love be never so unversed
that I would ever ask him first.
He ought to hold me far more dear.
Lord, since I shall not make it clear,
how could he know what I have felt?
What suffering I have been dealt
has not yet reached such an extent
to justify such loud lament.
I'll wait till he perceives it so,
1010   for I shall never let him know.
But if he ever were receptive
to Love, then he will be perceptive,
or learned of Love by spoken word.
Learned? What I've spoken is absurd.
For Love is not so kind and gracious
that one grows wise by words loquacious
without some good experience,
which personally I know makes sense.
For what I learned by flattery
1020   and hearsay was futility,
yet I was very long at school
where flattery has been the rule
and yet have always kept my distance.
Love makes me pay for my resistance;
I've learned more than an ox of plowing!*
One thing in this man I find cowing:
love he perhaps has been above;
if he loved not and does not love,
then in the ocean I have sown,

a place where seed cannot be grown,   1030
no more than seed can grow in ash.
Therefore I must endure Love's lash
and give him hints by word and sign
till he is sure of love of mine,
if he dares seek it once it's known.
There's no more save I am his own
and love him. If it is his whim
to love me not, I shall love him."
Thus he and she lament, conceal
from one another what they feel,   1040
and have bad days and nights more strained.
In my own view, they long remained
in Brittany, sad and distressed,
until the end of summer pressed.

ENGLAND AND KNIGHTHOOD

AT the beginning of October
came messengers by way of Dover
from London and from Canterbury
to give the king a commentary
on news that filled his heart with dread.
The king, the messengers now said,   1050
had stayed in Brittany too long.
For regent he had chosen wrong.
His land was now cause for dispute
with one who'd managed to recruit
from lands and friends a mighty host,
entrenched in London as his post,
to hold the town and keep it turned
against the king when he returned.
At this, the king, in rage and spite,
called all his barons, lord and knight.   1060

[31]

To make their willingness the greater
to cause the downfall of the traitor,
which he desired, he criticized
the course of action they'd advised
and told them that he blamed them for
his tribulation and his war:
they'd counseled him to grant his land
and place it in a felon's hand
who was far worse than Ganelon.*
1070   The lords conceded, every one,
the king was right in his reaction.
They had advised this course of action,
but now the man would be brought down.
Know well no citadel or town
would serve his body as redoubt,
for truly they would force him out,
and so the king was well assured.
All swore to him and pledged their word
they'd place the traitor in his hands
1080   or nevermore retain their lands.
Through Brittany the king had cried
none who could bear arms at his side
within an army should remain
but promptly come and join his train.
All Brittany directly stirred;
such legion never had occurred
as that King Arthur now amassed.
The fleet set sail and was so vast,
it seemed the world had gone to sea;
1090   the waves impossible to see,
for ships concealed them like a curtain.
This war was to be waged for certain.
At sea, the turmoil seemed to prove
all Brittany was on the move.
The crossing now already past,

the people from the ships, amassed,
took lodging places on the coast.
Then Alexander thought foremost
to go and ask the king outright
to be invested as a knight.   1100
If ever he would win acclaim,
this land would be where he won fame,
and his companions too were brought.
On doing what he willed and thought
he now was totally intent,
so he approached the royal tent.
The king was by his tent, outdoors.
He saw his Grecian visitors
and had them summoned to come near.
He said, "Lords, you must make it clear   1110
what reason motivates your call?"
So Alexander spoke for all
and told the king of his desire.
He said, "I've come to ask you, sire,
as I should ask of my own lord,
for knighthood, which, I pray, accord
to my companions and to me."
The king said, "Very willingly.
We shall proceed with all due speed.
Since you have asked me, I accede."   1120
The king required accoutrement
for thirteen knights brought to his tent,
and it was done at his command.
Each wanted gear; from the king's hand
he got equipment in due course,
fine weapons, and a sturdy horse.
Each took the gear made his to claim.
Now, for the twelve, all cost the same,
horse, garments, and accoutrement.
Their value was equivalent   1130

to Alexander's gear alone.
To sell or price, its worth outshone
the gear of all the twelve, equipped.
Right at the sea, the young men stripped,
and their ablutions were performed.
They deigned to have no water warmed
and wished for none to bathe and scrub.
They made the sea their bath and tub.
The queen learned, and she felt no hate
1140   for Alexander, of high rate
in her esteem and in her favor.
She wished to do him a great favor,
one greater than she thought to offer.
She searched and emptied chest and coffer
until at last she brought to light
a silk chemise, well made and white,
fine, delicate work to behold,
and only stitched in thread of gold
or at the least a silver strand.
1150   Now, Soredamors had lent a hand
from time to time in sewing it.
In places she had sewn a bit
of hair she'd taken from her head
at sleeves and neck, beside that thread,
just to determine and to learn
if that man lived who could discern
the difference where they were combined,
whom in this manner she might find.
The hair was light as gold and shone
1160   with equal or more lustrous tone.
To Alexander she conveyed
the shirt that Soredamors had made.
How joyful, Lord! would he have been
if he had known what gift the queen
was sending him to be his own.
The one whose hair therein was sewn

would have been joyful if aware
it would become her friend's to wear.
She would have been much comforted.
For all the hair left on her head   1170
she would not have felt fondness grander
than for the hair for Alexander,
but neither one knew it was so.
It's most distressing they don't know.
The messenger came from the queen,
and, where the youths were getting clean
at port, he found the youth aswim,
and so he gave the shirt to him.
The young man thought it beautiful
and held the gift more dearly still   1180
since it was at the queen's behest.
Had Alexander known the rest,
he would have loved it even more;
by it he would have set such store
he would not trade the world entire
in an exchange for his attire   1186
but as a relic, if I'm right,   a
he would adore it day and night.   b
Then Alexander straightaway   1187
attired himself in his array.
When dressed and with accoutrement
he went up to the monarch's tent   1190
with his companions in a throng.
The queen herself had come along
to sit therein, it seems to me,
because the queen desired to see
the new-made knights as they came in.
Their handsomeness was genuine,
but Alexander, straight and tall,
appeared the handsomest of all.
Now they were knights; enough's been said.

1200

I'LL tell about the king instead
and army that reached London town.
While most folk sided with the crown,
against him was a multitude,
for Count Angrès grouped men he wooed
by promises and gifts to sway
whomever he could turn his way.
When he had grouped his men to fight,
he fled in secrecy by night;
he was much hated and afraid

1210

that many wanted him betrayed.
Before he fled and left by stealth,
what he could seize of London's wealth,
its gold and silver, food, and stores,
he split among his warriors.
The news was given to the king
the traitor and his following
had taken flight, and all his force
had taken so much food by force
and city's wealth along their route

1220

the burghers now were destitute,
impoverished, and suffering.
He'd take no ransom, said the king,
none ever, for the traitor's head;
he'd have him hanged till he was dead
should once his prisoner he prove.
The army all got on the move
and on to Windsor made its way.
However the castle is today,
it was no easy residence

1230

to take because of its defense.
The traitor fortified the spot,
once he devised his treacherous plot,

with moats and with two walls, well backed
against collapsing when attacked,
with logs and stakes cut sharp and pointed.
The fortifying he appointed
for Windsor had been great in cost:
all June, July, and August lost
upon the tree-trunk palisades,
the drawbridge, barriers, barricades   1240
with ditches and with moats amid,
iron portcullises that slid,
and an enormous dressed-stone tower.*
No gate was closed at any hour
against assault or fear of foes.
On a high hill the castle rose;
below the flowing Thames was spied.
The army camped by riverside.
That day they would not have their fight
but pitched their tents to lodge the night   1250
and camped along the Thames's bed.
Their tents of green and golden red
filled all the meadow on that day.
The sunlight brought these hues in play;
they blazed along the river shore
for one full league and even more.
The castle knights came as a prank
to tourney on the gravel bank
with only lances that they grasped
and shields against their chests held clasped;   1260
they brought no other weapons down.
They showed the men outside the town
they held their troops in little fear,
because they came unarmed so near.
Then Alexander, on his side,
took notice of the knights who vied
on their bank in mock tournament.

To fight with them he was intent,
so he called each companion's name,
1270   one, then another, and they came.
First Cornix, whom he held so dear;
bold Licorides next came near,
then Nebunal the Mycenian,
Acorionde the Athenian,
and Ferolin of Salonica,
and Calcedor from Africa,
Parmenides and Francagel,
Torin the Strong, and Pinabel,
Nerius, and Neriolis.
1280   "My lords," he said, "my wish is this,
for those whose jousting is but show:
let's go and make them get to know
acquaintances like lance and shield,
for their contempt is unconcealed.
They must consider me no prize
as fighter, come before our eyes
disarmed completely for mock fight.
As yet to quintain or to knight
no first gift have we Grecians made
1290   upon our new-won accolade,
and our first lances, new, uncracked,
we have preserved too long intact.
Were our shields to be merely token?
As yet they are not pierced or broken,
possessions that aren't worth their salt
except for combat or assault.
Let's go for them across the ford."
Each said, "So help me God our Lord,
we shall not fail you in this end;
1300   who lets you down is not your friend."
All girded on their swords like lightning
and saddled up, their girth-straps tightening,

got mounted, and their shields were flung
around their necks. When shields were hung,
each seized his lance, whose hue was nice,
its paint was like its knight's device,
and toward the ford began to ride.
The people on the other side
went out to strike them, lances low,
but each Greek proved a worthy foe   1310
who'd not refuse to fight or yield
one single foot of battlefield.
Unsparing, each Greek struck his man;
none proved such an equestrian
that he stayed balanced on his mount.
The Greeks did not prove ones to count
mere boys, poor fighters, or deranged,
because the first blows they exchanged
weren't wasted: thirteen were unhorsed.
Within the army outcries coursed   1320
about their swordplay and their blows.
What brawl would follow, had their foes
dared wait for backers on Greek flanks,
who ran for weapons through the ranks,
then struck at Windsor with so dread
a clamor each opponent fled
and would not linger at the ford.
The Greeks struck out with lance and sword;
in hot pursuit of them they left,
with many heads cut off and cleft,   1330
but not a single Greek was hurt.   a
That day, their efforts were expert,   b
but Alexander led his band,   1331
for he tied up and took in hand
four knights, while other dead lay scattered,
and many were beheaded, battered,
or injured seriously, or maimed.

[39]

So Alexander, who had claimed
his first rewards of chivalry,
made them the queen's, from courtesy,
He wished to make the queen this present
1340 because he knew, and found unpleasant,
if they were in another's thrall,
the king would quickly hang them all.
On charge of treason, her decision
1344 was to have these knights held in prison.
a About the Greeks the army spoke,
b and Alexander, said these folk,
c was courteous and wise in thought
d about the knights whom he had caught.
e The king did not get those he won;
f he would have hanged them, every one.
1345 The unamused king sent for her*
to come at once and to confer.
She must not give his traitors cover;
the queen must either turn them over
to him or else be in defiance
1350 when he insisted on compliance.
The queen came, as appropriate,
and they discussed the traitors' fate;
what one another had in mind.
The Greeks had all remained behind
to talk with maids in the queen's tent.
The twelve were very eloquent,
but Alexander spoke no word.
Then Soredamors saw what occurred;
she sat beside him, close at hand.
1360 He had his chin within his hand,
and he appeared extremely pensive.
The time they sat became extensive.
At length she started to perceive
the hair beside his neck and sleeve

that she had sewn where they were edged.
A little closer now she edged.
She had a topic in that trim
on which she could converse with him,
but did not know which way was best
to start when he was first addressed. 1370
What opening word should she choose, a
or would his name be best to use? b
With her own self the maid conversed. 1371
She wondered: "What shall I say first?
Should I call him by name or try
to call him friend? Friend? No, not I.
What else then? Call him by his name!
But, Heavens! 'friend' is sweet to name.
'Friend' sounds so lovely and so caring.
I'd call him friend, were I so daring.
So daring? Why do I not try?
It's that I think that I would lie. 1380
A lie? I don't know what should be.
To tell a lie would weigh on me.
It would be best if I admit
that I do not think lying fit.
He would not lie, the Lord forfend!
if he should call me his sweet friend.
Then would I lie about this youth?
The two of us should tell the truth.
Were I to lie, I'd be to blame.
Why wish he had another name? 1390
Why does his put my tongue in fetters?
I think it has too many letters.
I'd stutter to a stop midway,
while 'friend' is easier to say.
That is a name I could say fast;
the other name I can't get past,
so my own blood I would expend

if his real name were 'my sweet friend.'"
So long had Soredamors sojourned
1400   in thoughts like these, the queen returned
from where the king had her appear.
When Alexander saw her near,
he went to meet and ask the queen
just what the king's command had been
about his prisoners and their end.
She said, "He has required me, friend,
to place the four knights at his will
for punishment for doing ill.
He's angry I did not allow
1410   these captives to be his by now,
so I must send along my prize.
He wants them brought before his eyes."
So that was how that day was passed,
and on the morrow there amassed
before the king's pavilion royal
the knights who had proved good and loyal
to say, by judgment and by law,
what painful deaths these four would draw,
imposed by those they had betrayed.
1420   Some knights declared they should be flayed,
and others wished them hanged or burned.
The king himself said those who turned
to treason should be drawn apart.*
This penalty he did impart.
He had them fetched; he had them bound
and said they would be drawn around
the castle walls, and all inside
could watch and see the way they died.
Once he pronounced the penalty,
1430   the king, who wished them panicky,
went into the great palace hall.
There Alexander, at his call,

came and was called the king's dear friend.
"Friend, I was watching you contend,
assail, and parry yesterday,
and I must give to you in pay
five hundred Welsh knights for your band
and men-at-arms from my own land,
so you will be one thousand more.
When I have finished with my war,   1440
besides this much for your travails
I'll give the finest realm in Wales.
As king I'll have you wear its crown,
with city, castle, hall, and town.
I'll make it yours until the land
your father holds in his command,
of which you shall be emperor,
is yours as its inheritor."
Then Alexander was most swift
to thank the king for such a gift,   1450
and his companions said their thanks.
At court the barons of all ranks
said Alexander had been graced
by kingly gifts that were well placed.
When Alexander saw his men,
his boon companions, his armed men,
the men the king would make his own,
throughout the army he had blown
the bugle horns' and trumpets' call.
The brave and craven, one and all,   1460
took up their arms, no one did not,
and, Welsh and British, Cornish, Scot,
they represented a great force.
The army had been raised, of course,
from every quarter in its number.
Because it had not rained all summer,
the Thames had fallen in its bed,

so in the river fish were dead
because of the tremendous drought;
1470   boats lay aground within the port.*
So where the river was most wide
it could be forded side to side.
Across the Thames the army spilled;
part sought the valley, which they filled;
part sought the hill and made the climb.
The castle guard saw them in time.
They saw the wondrous army come,
preparing ways to overcome
the castle and to take it back,
1480   so they prepared for the attack.
Before the start of the assault,
the traitors suffered for their fault.
The king placed them at horses' tails
and had them dragged around the vales
encircling the castle round,
and over hills and fallow ground.
Then Count Angrès felt choler rise
to see them drawn before his eyes,
whom he had held so very dear.
1490   The other men were filled with fear,
but even though their fear was great,
they'd no wish to capitulate.
The king had shown his rage and spleen,
and everyone had clearly seen,
if they were caught and ceased to vie,
what shameful deaths he'd make them die.
A new offense began to start,
now that the four were drawn apart,
and in the field their limbs lay tossed.
1500   Yet all their laboring was lost:
they hurled and shot at those inside
without success, although they tried.

They hurled and shot at those within
with stone and dart and javelin;
a fracas was the end result
of crossbow and of catapult.
Round stones and arrows that were cast
flew through the air as thick and fast
as hailstones falling mixed with rain,
and all sides joined in this campaign.   1510
All day their effort was intense;
some on attack, some on defense,
until night parted those who vied.
Upon his side the king had cried
what royal gift he would bestow,
so all his troops would come to know,
on him to whom the castle fell:
"A cup that's very valuable,
of fifteen marks of gold, as fee,
the richest in my treasury."   1520
The precious cup would be ornate,
and, the unvarnished truth to state,
in cost, the workmanship displayed
surpassed the gold of which it's made,
and, though it was superior,
the gems on the exterior
were valued, if the truth were told,
above the workmanship and gold.
A man-at-arms who took the keep
would have the golden cup to keep.   1530
A knight who pierced through its defense
might ask for any recompense,
besides the cup, that could be found
and furnished in the whole world's bound.
When this announcement had been cried,
as Alexander'd not let slide
his custom every evenfall

[45]

to pay the queen an evening call,
there, on that evening, he was seen.
1540
So Alexander and the queen
sat side by side, together thrown,
while Soredamors, who sat alone,
was nearest to them and in face.
She gazed at Alexander's face,
a pleasure that she found so nice,
she did not wish for Paradise.
The queen held Alexander's hand,
his right one, and meanwhile she scanned
the golden thread, which was much tarnished.
1550
The hair seemed lovelier, more burnished;
the golden thread was now outshone.
That Soredamors thereon had sewn
the queen remembered by some chance
and laughed at the significance.
So Alexander asked her after
if she would tell what caused her laughter,
but, hesitant to tell its source,
the queen regarded Soredamors
and spoke a summons to come near,
1560
which Soredamors was pleased to hear.
She came before the queen and knelt.
What pleasure Alexander felt
to see her come so close at hand
he could have touched her with his hand,
but was not bold enough to dare
to look upon her kneeling there.
His wits all fled once she had come,
so he was stricken nearly dumb.
Such disconcertment overtook
1570
the maid, she knew not where to look.
Too much abashed to glance around,
she only stared down at the ground.

The queen, astonished at the sight,
watched Soredamors turn red and white
and pondered in her heart the air
and countenance shown by the pair,
first separately, then both combined.
The truth seemed certain to her mind:
the changing colors of complexion
had love as cause and as connection.   1580
She did not want the two upset
or to appear to know as yet
what she had managed to detect.
The queen's behavior was correct,
and so she kept her face a blank,
except she told the maid, "Be frank,
do look here, maid, and make it known
about where this chemise was sewn
this knight is wearing on his back,
and hold no portion of it back   1590
if you took part or put a bit   a
of something of your own in it."   b
She scalded with embarrassment,   1591
yet told the truth and was content
because she wanted him to hear.
When she replied and made it clear
the way the white chemise was wrought,
he was so joyous at the thought
that when he looked upon the hair*
it took great effort to forbear
from falling down upon his knees
and worshipping the white chemise.   1600
He felt displeasure that was keen
that his companions and the queen
were also present; otherwise
he'd touch the shirt to mouth and eyes
most willingly, but he believed

[47]

his gesture would have been perceived.
Though glad of so much of his friend,
he did not think that in the end
he would have any more of her.
1610   Desire has made him insecure.
One hundred thousand times, at ease,
1612   and more, he kissed the white chemise,
a   when on the queen he ceased to wait,
b   and felt he was born fortunate,
1613   and he rejoiced throughout the night,
though careful to be out of sight.
When lying on his bed at leisure,
he took a vain delight and pleasure
where there was no delight to taste.
All night he held the shirt embraced.
He gazed upon that tiny strand
1620   and felt the world his to command.
Love turns the wise to fools most rare
when one rejoices at one hair;
he'll make a change in that delight.
Delight filled Alexander's night.
Before bright dawn and light of sun
the traitors' council had begun
about what options could be planned.
They knew they long could keep in hand
the castle, that was a sure thing,
1630   by stout defense against the king.
His will, however, was so strong
and obstinate, his whole life long
he would not leave the citadel
or turn aside until it fell.
They could expect no mercy rendered;
they'd surely die if they surrendered
and gave the castle back to him,
1638   so their alternatives were grim,

for here and there no comfort lies,   a
and here and there looms their demise.   b
Yet from their counsels it emerged   1639
next day, before the daybreak verged,   1640
they'd leave the castle bounds concealed
and find the army in the field,
by arms and armor unencumbered,
while in their beds the knights still slumbered.
Before they woke from sleep and slipped
their armor on and were equipped,
the massacre wrought by the slayers
would keep the deeds of these betrayers
that evening evermore alive.
Since they despaired they would survive,   1650
the traitors all placed their reliance
upon this counsel from defiance.
Thus desperation, come what may,
made them emboldened for the fray.
They saw no way to circumvent
their deaths or their imprisonment.
A poor solution did they scrape,
nor was it worthwhile to escape.
They did not see where they could flee.
The water and their enemy   1660
enclosed the traitors all around
and kept them in the middle, bound.
The traitors from their council slipped;
at once they armed and got equipped.
They went out to retaliate
northwest through an old postern gate;   1666
they thought the army least prepared   a
for them to choose the way they fared.   b
In serried ranks, their men divided   1667
and formed five companies, provided
each with two thousand men-at-arms

1670   equipped for battle, bearing arms,
and knights, one thousand per brigade.
That night no moon or star displayed
its shining rays high in the skies,
but then the moon began to rise
before the traitors reached the tents.
I think, to do them violence*
the moon arose before its time,
and God, to harm them for their crime,
illuminated the dark night,
1680   not caring for their army's plight
but hating them, and for the reason
that they were soiled by sin of treason.
God feels more hate for treachery
than any other felony.
So God ordained the moon to shine
so that the moon would be malign.
The moon was most malign to beam
upon their shields and make them gleam.
Their helmets added to their plight
1690   by shining with reflected light.
The sentries who were keeping watch
could see the traitors on the march
and through the army raised the shout:
"Get up at once, knights, up and out,
and get your weapons out and arm.
Here come the traitors bent on harm!"
Throughout the army arms were drawn;
men strove to put their weapons on,
as they must do in such great need.
1700   Not one man started to proceed
until he'd armed himself, unhurried.
All mounted. Meanwhile, traitors scurried,
while they were arming at their pace,
and eagerly began to race

to catch the army by surprise
and take them still in unarmed guise.
The army saw these men in sections
approaching them from five directions.
Close to the woodland one group kept;
along the river one group crept.   1710
Inside the woodland went the third;
the fourth, a valley; the fifth spurred
on through a cutting in a rock
where they believed that, with no block,
they could rush freely through the tents.*
The king's men mounted a defense;
so as that company came near,
they did not find the passage clear.
Fierce challenges as they approached
were spoken, and they were reproached   1720
that their disloyalty prevailed.
With iron lance tips they assailed   1722
each other till all lances split,   a
then turned to swords, collided, hit   b
so they made one another sprawl   c
face down as they kept up their brawl.   d
They sought each other in the fray   1723
and ran as lions run for prey
and then devour all that they catch.
Their fierceness was at least a match.
That first assault, to tell you true,
left both sides many deaths to rue.
The traitors, mounting fierce resistance,
obtained additional assistance.   1730
The price was high when lives were sold,
but when they could no longer hold,
the traitors saw their other sections
arriving there from four directions
to give them aid in their defense.

The king's men mounted an offense.
As fast as they could spur they raced;
on traitors' shields such blows were placed,
five hundred men they overthrew
1740 and more, the wounded counted too.
The Greeks spared none; nor, as he fought,
was Alexander lost in thought.
He strove for excellent swordplay.
He sought the thickest of the fray
and went to strike a worthless glutton
who was not even worth a button;
the mail and shield within his grip
weren't worth a dark blue silken strip.
When Alexander gave him truce,
1750 he offered to a traitor's use
his service without loss or waste.
He struck so viciously in haste
from corpse he ousted soul and ghost
and left the hostel with no host.
With these two down, he started dashing
toward a third knight, wellborn and dashing.
He struck through both flanks when they vied,
so blood sprang out the other side,
and from the corpse the soul retired,
1760 which he breathed out as he expired.
Thus, like a flying thunderbolt,
he slaughtered many in revolt
and wounded many, for he flew
so fast at those he hurt and slew
no mail or shield was guarantee,
and his companions were as free
with blood and brains they spread about.
They knew how blows should be dealt out.
The king's men battled and coerced.
1770 Their foes broke up and were dispersed

[52]

like senile men with wits astray.
So many dead in ploughed fields lay,
so many hours the fight went on
that even well before the dawn
the battle was so turbulent
the dead lay in a line that went
for five leagues down the riverbanks.
Then Count Angrès dropped in the ranks
his banner and rode at an amble.
Of his companions in his gamble   1780
he took but seven and rode back
to reach his castle by a track
so hidden that he could believe
that nobody had seen them leave.
But Alexander saw the group
steal off and flee the major troop.
If he could slip away unseen,
he'd meet with those who left the scene.
He saw, before he reached the vale,
some thirty knights upon his trail   1790
who'd noted his attempt to sneak.
Two dozen Welsh, six others Greek,
who thought to follow at a distance
so they could come to his assistance,
for that was what they had in mind.
When he observed them far behind,
then Alexander stopped to wait.
Then he began to cogitate
and note which way those who returned
to Windsor Castle's walls had turned,   1800
until he saw the traitors enter.
He thought of an audacious venture,
an idea dangerous to use,
a wonderfully clever ruse,
and after he had thought it through,

the closer Alexander drew
to his companions, whom he told
about his scheme that was so bold.
"Lords, grant my wishes unopposed
1810   if you would keep me well disposed,
be it a wise or foolish deed."
They would not challenge, they agreed,
what Alexander would arrange.
"Now our insignia we'll change
by carrying a lance and shield
borne by the traitors here revealed.
We will go toward the castle thus.
The traitors will believe of us
that we are allies on their side.
1820   Then, come whatever may betide,
within they'll open up the gate.
What way shall we reciprocate?
In turn, once we have gone ahead,
we'll take them all, alive or dead,
if Heaven grants they can be caught.
If any has one second thought,
my whole life long I shall impart
no love for him with a true heart."
They all accorded what he pleased.
1830   They sought the dead men's shields and seized
and put on their accoutrements.
Within the keep, to battlements,
the castle knights had climbed on high.
The shields they could identify
and took them for their own men's use,
for they did not suspect the ruse
that shields concealed invaders' traits.
The porter opened up the gates,
admitted them, and in they trooped.
1840   The porter was deceived and duped;

[54]

when they came in, he did not speak,
and not a word said Welsh or Greek.
All mute and still, they made belief
and managed such a show of grief
they dragged their lances down behind
and, bending over shields, they pined
and seemed to grieve and to lament.
Then, anywhere they wished, they went;
there were three walls* through which they passed.
Up there they found armed men amassed   1850
and knights together with the count.
I cannot tell you their true count,
but none of them were armor-clad
excepting eight, those men who had
slipped from the ranks to the redoubt,
and these eight men were just about
to take off their accoutrement.
Such hastiness they might repent,
for the invaders who had ridden
no longer kept their faces hidden   1860
but came upon them. Feet were set
firm in the stirrups as they met.
Attacking, letting chargers run,
they executed twenty-one
before a challenge was made heard.
The traitors, stunned by what occurred,
were shouting out, "Betrayed! Betrayed!"
But the assailants weren't afraid,
because their swords had been well tried
on those who'd laid their arms aside;   1870
moreover, they had been so charmed
with three whom they encountered armed
that they let only five men live.
Then Count Angrès rushed out to give
a blow upon the shield of gold

of Macedor all could behold,
so that he struck him dead to ground.
His wrath and grief, which were profound,
at seeing his companion slain

1880
drove Alexander near insane.
His blood was boiling in his trouble,
and yet his strength and nerve grew double.
He went to deal the count a stroke
so furious his wood lance broke,
for if he could, within one breath
he'd have revenge for his friend's death.
But Count Angrès was full of might,
a bold and an accomplished knight.
Had he not been a wicked traitor,

1890
no knight on earth would have been greater.
The count responded with a blow
that bent his lance into a bow
until it quivered and it cracked,
and yet the shield remained intact,
and neither knight budged from the shock,
not any more than would a rock,
for both of them were very strong.
The fact the count was in the wrong
became his great impediment.

1900
Both knights drew out their swords and went
for one another with swordplay.
They'd smashed their lances in their fray.
There would have been no help for it,
if these two craftsmen had seen fit
to fight on longer and contend;
soon one would bring it to an end,
whoever did so, at the last.
And yet the count dared not stand fast;
around him, taken by surprise,

1910
he saw his unarmed men's demise.

The fierce invading force attacked;
they cut and tonsured, carved and whacked,
and, as they battled on and shrilled,
"The count's a traitor!" brains were spilled.
When charged with treason, in so deep,
he ran for refuge to the keep,
and with the count his people fled.
Their foes escorted them ahead;
in fierce pursuit of them they raced.
Of all they captured when they chased   1920
they let no man escape, not one,
and such a massacre was done
just seven, I believe no more,
survived to reach the refuge door.
The count's men reached the keep, at bay,
and halted at the entry way,
for those who followed on their route
had come so close in hot pursuit
that if the entry way were free,
they would have entered instantly.   1930
The traitors fought those who attacked,
for they expected to be backed;
their men were arming down in town.
A Greek with wisdom of renown
named Nebunal told their patrol
to keep each passage in control,
so that fresh help could not arrive.
They had delayed from lack of drive
and cowardice until too late.
There was one single entrance gate   1940
to reach the castle's upper ward,
and if that opening were barred,
no evil would they have to fear
from any forces coming near.
So Nebunal said, "Separate

[57]

some twenty men to hold the gate
against some reinforcing force
that soon, if it had power or force
to penetrate that walled defense,
1950   would strike and do them violence.
Let twenty hold the gate closed fast;
let ten before the keep door, massed,
assault the count in that redoubt
from whence he sought to close them out."
They did as Nebunal thought right:
before the keep ten stayed to fight,
and to the gate went twenty strong,
who'd almost waited overlong.
They saw a band of infantry,
1960   inflamed for fresh hostility,
with archers with crossbows to wind
and men-at-arms of every kind
with weaponry of every like.
Some men-at-arms had brought the pike,
while others bore the Danish ax
or Turkish sword in their attacks,
or lance or javelin, dart or bolt.
Faced with these backers of revolt,
the Greeks and Welshmen would have lost
1970   and had to leave at heavy cost,
but they came to the count's defense
too late, and by the wisdom, sense,
and counsel Nebunal disbursed
the twenty closed the gateway first.
Outside the ward the troops reposed,
once that the entry way was closed.
They clearly saw that to assail
the ward would be of no avail.
Each woman, small child, youth, old man
1980   within the castle wall began

such lamentation, such loud cries,
had there been thunder in the skies,
the castle knights would not have heard.
The Greeks rejoiced, all now assured
there was no chance the count could flee
except into captivity.
Of Alexander's bold offense
four swiftly scaled the battlements
and solely to watch from the heights
lest those without at any sites   1990
have some device or stratagem
to bring the castle down on them.
The other sixteen of his men
returned and joined the fighting ten.
It was broad day, the sun was out.
The ten had brought so much about
that they won entry to the keep.
The count, who had an ax to sweep,
had placed himself before a post
and was with self-defense engrossed.   2000
He fiercely swung his ax and strove;
whomever he could reach he clove.
His men were ranged beside him, fast,
obtaining vengeance to the last;
in nothing were their efforts feigned.
Then Alexander's men complained,
for they were down to thirteen men
and once had been sixteen and ten.
So Alexander, near insane
to see his men fatigued and slain   2010
and in such harm and weakened state,
moved swiftly to retaliate.
He found a rack, from which he stole
a long and heavy hanging pole.
He smashed it on a worthless glutton,

whose shield did not prove worth a button,
whose hauberk was of no more worth,
and felled his victim to the earth.
Then Alexander sought the count
2020   and raised the pole to make it count.
He dealt the count so hard a clout
the squared pole nearly knocked him out.
The ax fell from his hands upraised.
The count was left so stunned and dazed
his feet gave out, and, lest he fall,
he had to lean against the wall.
Upon that blow, the battle ceased,
and Alexander sprang and seized
the count, who neither stirred nor moved.
2030   The rest were easily removed
when they had seen their lord waylaid;
of them no mention shall be made.
With Count Angrès, so harshly served,
they were led off as they deserved,
arrested and in deep disgrace.
The royal troops outside the place
were unaware; when it was day,
at the conclusion of the fray,
the shields borne by the Greeks were found
2040   among the bodies on the ground.
Mistaken in their grief, the Greeks
mourned for their lord with anguished shrieks.
His shield, which all could recognize,
made them lament and agonize
and faint upon their shields and say
they rued they'd lived to see that day.
Cornix and Nerius revived,
regretting that they had survived;
Torin wept with Acorionde
2050   and life and joyfulness disowned.

[60]

With tears their eyes were so replete
they flowed like waves down to their feet.
Parmenides, whose deep despair
surpassed the others', tore his hair.
These five lamented for their lord
(no one could have been more deplored)
with grief that was unmerited.
They bore another in his stead
and thought their lord was being borne.
The other shields caused them to mourn;   2060
they thought the corpses thereby lain
were those of their companions, slain,
so all began to cry and faint.
But all the shields were but a feint.
One comrade, named Neriolis,
was all the dead that they would miss.
They could have borne his corpse alone,
if but the truth of it were known.
Yet they were equally distressed
about him and about the rest.   2070
Although the corpses all were taken,
in all but one they were mistaken,
but like a sleeping man who deems
a lie is truth when plunged in dreams,
the shields gave rise to a delusion,
and for the truth they took illusion.
Thus by the shields they were misled.
They moved away with all the dead,
and they proceeded to their tents,
where many people raised laments,   2080
but when the Greeks began their cry,
all other people gathered by;
a crowd assembled as they grieved.
Now, Soredamors thought and believed
herself to be unlucky born

to hear her friend was cause to mourn.
Her mourning and her grief began
to make her face turn pale and wan,
and that she did not dare reveal

2090   the grief the news had made her feel
was even more distress and smart.
She hid her sorrow in her heart.
Had anybody read her face,
her great distress left every trace
upon her physical appearance
at Alexander's disappearance,
but each one raised his own laments
with self-concern grown so intense
that he cared nothing for the rest.

2100   His private sorrow each expressed,
a   because the riverbank was covered
b   with friends and relatives discovered
c   destroyed and injured by their toss,
d   and each one mourned his private loss,
2101   to him a heavy, bitter one.
A father weeping for a son;
a son wept for a father dead;
one fainted where a cousin bled;
another for a nephew slain.
Thus fathers, sons, and kin in pain
in every place raised loud lament.
The Greeks' grief was so violent
it was most easy to detect,

2110   from which great joy they might expect.
The greatest grief felt armywide
soon by great joy will be belied.
Without, the Greeks were grieving hard,
while those within gave much regard
to any means they could employ
to tell the Greeks and bring them joy.

The prisoners, disarmed and tied,
beseeched their captors while inside
to cut their heads off on the spot.
Their captors deigned not and would not   2120
but said they'd keep them and would bring
and hand them over to the king,
who'd see they got what they deserved,
so they were quits and rightly served.
Disarming all in the redoubt
to show them to their troops without,
they took them to the battlements.
This kindness gave them deep offense;
they saw their lord a captive, bound,
and happiness did not abound.   2130
Then Alexander, on the wall,
swore by the Lord and His saints all
he would not leave one man alive.
Mass sudden death he would contrive
for all the captives in his string,
unless the troops fell to the king.
"As I command, go straightaway
to my lord king without delay
and throw yourself upon his grace.
No one deserves death in this place   2140
except the count and only him.
You shall not forfeit life or limb
if you cry to the king for quarter.
If you don't save yourself from slaughter
by seeking grace with that mere cry,
how little less can you rely
upon preserving life and hide.
Remove your armor, go outside,
and say before the king you came
from Alexander, in my name.   2150
You won't have wandered from your path.

[63]

For all his outrage and his wrath,
my lord the king will then see fit
to pardon you if you submit;
he is so gracious and so kind.
If you do other than my mind,
you're bound to die, for in no fashion
do I intend to show compassion."
To this advice all gave assent

2160 and went straight to the royal tent,
and at the royal feet fell prone.
Throughout the army it was known
what these men told him and recounted.
The king got mounted; all got mounted;
and toward the castle wall they spurred,
and so no more delay occurred.
Then Alexander, exiting
the castle, met the happy king
and handed over Count Angrès.

2170 The king brooked no more tardiness
in justly serving that commander
but praised and honored Alexander,
and all the other troops rejoiced.
Esteem and praise of him were voiced.
Each one rejoiced; joy drove away
the sorrowing and the dismay
that they had earlier expressed.
The Grecian joy surpassed the rest;
no other joy could measure up.

2180 The king presented him the cup
worth fifteen marks, ornate and rare,
and said he had no thing so fair
he cherished with desire so keen,
excepting for his crown and queen,
that he would not at once accord
to Alexander as reward.

[64]

But Alexander did not dare
say what he sought in this affair,
although he knew he could depend
on being granted his sweet friend,   2190
yet feared to ask lest he annoy
someone who would have felt sheer joy,
but he preferred to suffer still
than have her hand against her will,
and so he asked a bit of leisure
because, until he learned her pleasure,
he would not make his own request.
The golden cup he soon possessed;
with that no leisure need there be.   2199
He took the gift; with courtesy   a
he begged the lord Gawain accept   b
the cup from him, a gift he kept   c
but did reluctantly obey.   d

ALEXANDER'S WEDDING

WHEN Soredamors heard them convey   2200
    real news of Alexander's fate,
it put her in a blissful state,
and when she learned he was alive,
such joyfulness did she derive
from that good news, in her belief
she'd never have an hour of grief.
She found it long until he paid
the visit that he usually made.
She'll have her will in due course yet,
for one thing has them both beset,   2210
which one the more no one could measure.
How Alexander longed at leisure
To feast on one sweet look from her!

He had not wanted to defer
his visit to the queen's own tent,
but was detained and discontent
that he had suffered a delay.
As soon as he could get away,
straight to the queen's pitched tent he came.
2220 The queen met him and knew his frame
of mind and thinking in large part,
although he had not bared his heart,
and yet she clearly had perceived.
He entered and was well received.
The queen was very genial;
she well knew why he came to call.
She summoned Soredamors to her,
a further favor to confer.
So these three only got them hence,
2230 far from the rest, in conference.
The queen was first at speaking out,
for she had not the slightest doubt
their love was mutual and clear.
He held her, and she held him, dear.
She knew it firmly in her mind,
and Soredamors could never find
a better sweetheart than this man.
She sat between them and began
to share with them a line of reason
2240 that was in proper place and season.
"Now, Alexander, I would rate
love to be even worse than hate
when it gives friends distress and rue
and lovers know not what they do,
when they keep hidden what they feel,
for love takes effort, a good deal,
and is confusing and head-spinning.
Who fails to make a bold beginning

[66]

can hardly win the end result.
The first step is most difficult;   2250
the threshold worst to cross above.
I want to teach you two of Love,
for I see Love is being cruel.
I want to have you go to school.
Take care that nothing is concealed.
Your countenances have revealed
most clearly to me what you've done:
of two hearts you have fashioned one.
Do not conceal yourselves from me!
You each would act so foolishly,   2260
if you won't make your thinking plain.
Concealment leaves the other slain,
and you will both be Love's assassins.
I warn you, force and lustful passions
in love you must not seek or sate.
In marriage and in honored state
remain in mutual company,
and in this way, it seems to me,
the love you feel will long endure.
I promise, and you may be sure,   2270
if you're inclined toward matrimony,
I shall arrange the ceremony."
When once the queen made her thoughts known,
next Alexander voiced his own.
"My lady, I've no arguments
to offer you in self-defense.
I grant all you accuse me of
and never would be free of Love,
on which I'll always be intent.
I'm gratified and well content   2280
that you are speaking as you do.
Since my desire is known to you,
why I should hide it I don't know.

If I had dared to, long ago
I'd have admitted what I feel,
for it was grueling to conceal,
but it could be that in her mind
this maid is not the least inclined
to have me or to be my own.
2290   Though she may keep herself alone,
I give myself to her the same."
At these words trembling overcame
the maid, who'd not decline the gift.
Her heart's will and her feelings' drift
her words and signs did not dissemble.
She gave herself to him atremble,
and said that she was not inclined
to hold back body, heart, or mind,
for all of them, at his proposal,
2300   were wholly at the queen's disposal
to do her pleasure and none other.
The queen gave them to one another,
although first she embraced the two.
"Now, Alexander, I give you
the body of your dear sweetheart,
because I know you have her heart.
Whoever makes a fuss and bother,
I give you two to one another.
You take your own, and you take yours."
2310   He has his own, and she has hers.
He has her wholly, she him wholly.
At Windsor they did not move slowly.
With the approval and consent
the king and Sir Gawain both lent,
that day became their wedding day.
In a description, I should say,
of joy, delight in plenitude,
great opulence, delicious food

that wedding would have even more.
Since many would find me a bore,   2320
my words I do not wish to scatter;
I'll work on better subject matter.

THE BIRTH OF CLIGÈS

AT Windsor, in one single day,
such joy and honor did they pay
to Alexander as could be.
He had three joys and honors three:
one was the castle he had seized;
another, when the war had ceased,
King Arthur said he'd have the best
and finest kingdom Wales possessed;   2330
upon that day he would install
King Alexander in his hall.
And yet his third joy was most keen,
which was at chess his love was queen
upon the board where he was king.
Less than three months were finishing
when Soredamors was full indeed
of human grain and human seed,
a seed she carried to full term.*
The human seed remained in germ   2340
until the fruit appeared, in nature
a baby; near or far no creature
was found of greater handsomeness.
The little child was called Cligès.
This tale was written, to enhance
his memory, as a French romance.
Of him and how he did engage
in knightly feats when once of age,
so he could make himself a name,

2350   I'll tell you later of his aim.
But in the end, the realm of Greece
endured the emperor's decease.
Constantinople was his seisin.
He died, but in his proper season;
his life could not exceed its span.
He gathered every nobleman
within his land when he was smitten
and had them send and search in Britain
for Alexander, who had made

2360   a home there and had gladly stayed.
The messengers upon their trip
left Greece; their people and their ship
met with a storm that struck and tossed
both man and vessel; all were lost
and died by drowning in the sea,
save one rogue skilled at felony,*
whose love for young Alis was grander
than for the elder Alexander.
The rogue escaped from storm and wave,

2370   returned to Greece, and then the knave
reported all their company
were stricken by a storm at sea
as they returned from Britain's shore
to bring their lord to Greece once more.
He, sole survivor of them all,
escaped the perils and the squall.
The news this liar had disclosed
was never challenged or opposed.
They placed Alis upon the throne

2380   and made the empire Greece his own.
The news reached Alexander's shore,
and he soon learned the emperor
was now Alis and no one other.
His land unchallenged to his brother

thus Alexander would not leave,
so of King Arthur he took leave.
The king in no way thought him wrong
but said he ought to take along
so large an army, filled with lots
of Welshmen, Cornishmen, and Scots,   2390
his brother would not dare stand fast
once he had seen his host amassed.

ALEXANDER'S SETTLEMENT

THOUGH Alexander could set course
to Greece and take a mighty force,
he was in hopes he could avoid
a fight that would leave Greeks destroyed,
if his young brother would comply
with what he wished and so reply.
He took with him knights forty strong
and Soredamors and son along.   2400
By love they were so intertwined
he would not leave those two behind.
Once they all took leave of the court,
they put to sea at Shoreham port.
The ship ran like a fleeing stag
upon fair winds; in one month's lag
they put into the port before
strong Athens with its wealthy store.
The emperor was in residence
within that town, and an immense   2410
assembly of the noblemen,
the country's lords, had gathered then.
A friend went out on their return,
whom Alexander sent to learn
what, in the city, was believed:

[71]

could Alexander be received,
or would the city not accord
he was their true and rightful lord?
His friend was Ariconde by name.
2420   This knightly messenger who came
had wisdom, courtesy, eloquence,
and property in affluence.
The country thought him great in worth,
for Athens was his place of birth.
Within the city, by tradition,
his ancestry held high position;
high office his ancestors owned.
Once it was known to Ariconde
the emperor was in the town,
2430   he'd challenge him about the crown
for Alexander, his own brother.
This knight would not forgive another
who had unlawfully been crowned.
He went straight to the palace, found
well-wishers pleased he had come by,
but Ariconde would not reply
to any man or say one word
to any greeting that he heard.
He acted thus till he could find
2440   what were their plans and state of mind
toward their true lord, so he forbore
and went straight to the emperor.
He did not hail him, would not bow
or call him emperor even now.
"Alis," he said, "I bring report
from Alexander in the port.
Hear what your brother would have known,
for he now asks you for his own,
and he asks nothing to excess.
2450   Constantinople you possess;

he is and ought to be its lord.
Between you should be no discord;
dissention is not right or fit.
Take my advice, agree on it.
Give him the crown without a fight;
you should surrender it by right."
Alis responded, "My dear friend,
this message-bearing you intend
is on your part an act of folly,
no comfort in my melancholy.   2460
My brother's dead," was his retort.
"I don't believe he's at the port.
If he were living, and I knew,
I never would believe it true
until I saw that it was so;
I grieve he died some time ago.
I credit nothing you have said.
Why won't he come if he's not dead?
He'd rest assured that I would hand
to him a large expanse of land.   2470
If he keeps from me, he's a dolt.
The crown and empire, in revolt,
none will hold from me; in reverse,
he'd serve me and be none the worse."
When Ariconde had heard him clear,
he did not hesitate from fear
to voice his views and his protests.
"Confound me if the matter rests,
Alis, and I defy your claim,"
he told him, "in your brother's name,   2480
on his behalf, as I must do.
To come to him and part from you
I summon all here at your court.
They ought to lend him their support
and rightly make him their liege lord.

Let those who will be true come forward."
He left the court upon that word.
In turn, the emperor conferred
with those in whom he placed reliance
2490   about his brother's stout defiance.
He sought advice, to comprehend
if he could trust them not to lend
support and give his brother aid
in this resistance he had made.
He wished to test each one at court,
but none of them would lend support
in this war to the emperor.
All told him to recall the war
that one time Polynices waged
2500   with Eteocles and so engaged
as enemy his own full brother,
and each one died slain by the other.*
They said, "The same could be your end;
if he wants war and will contend,
the land will suffer ravishment."
They opted for a settlement,
fair, rational, with neither brother
requiring too much of the other.
Alis, if he would not contract
2510   and give his brother a fair pact,
learned all his lords would leave his side.
He said he'd properly abide
by any pact they might submit
but specified they must commit,
whatever terms might be laid down,
that he, Alis, would keep the crown.
To make a firm peace, a commander
went from Alis to Alexander
to bid him come; the land in whole
2520   would henceforth be in his control;

Alis would keep this much renown:
the title emperor and crown.
If he found this exclusion fair,
peace would be made between the pair.
When this proposal was recounted
to Alexander, his men mounted,
to Athens they began to ride,
and when in Athens, at his side,
they all were joyously received.
But Alexander felt aggrieved;   2530
in great displeasure he demurred
when this proposal had been heard.
His brother would not be allowed
to keep the crown unless he vowed
he would not marry evermore.
Cligès would be next emperor
of Constantinople and succeed.
And thus the brothers were agreed,
for Alexander swore his oath;
Alis gave him his pledge of both   2540
control and never in his life
to take a woman as his wife.
They were agreed; friends they remained.
The barons' joy was unrestrained.
They had Alis for emperor,
but great and small things came before
his brother, and in every one
what Alexander said was done.
Without him, little was achieved.
All Emperor Alis received   2550
was that high title he conserved,
with Alexander loved and served.
Who did not serve from love sincere
served Alexander out of fear.
Through love and fear he did command

and rule at will throughout the land.
But nonetheless the one called Death
deprives all men of life and breath
and spares no man, infirm or spry;
2560 so Alexander had to die.
A malady gripped him secure
for which there could be found no cure.
Death overtook him suddenly,
but first he made his son this plea:
"You'll never know, dear son, Cligès,
your worth in skill and stalwartness
unless first at King Arthur's court
you demonstrate how you comport
yourself exchanging blow and stroke
2570 with Britons and with English folk.
Now, should adventure take you there,
conduct yourself with such good care
you are not recognized by name
until you prove that you can claim
a place at court among the best.
Believe me; do as I request.
Should such occasion be dispensed,
don't fear to test yourself against
your uncle, who is Sir Gawain.
2580 I pray this counsel you'll retain."
He did not long survive this plea.
Next Soredamors, intensively,
felt grief so terrible and grim
that she could not live after him;
she died with him of woefulness.
Thereon Alis mourned with Cligès
for Alexander, properly,
2588 but then they let their mourning be,
a for every grief one must transcend,
b and all that comes to pass must end.

Long mourning has no benefit, 2589
because no good can come of it. 2590
Their mourning ended for his life.

A GERMAN MARRIAGE

THE emperor first took no wife;
for lengthy years he stayed unwed
and loyal to the vow he'd said.
But there's no court the world around
where bad advice cannot be found.
Such bad advice can often sway
the lords and make them go astray,
so they abandon loyalty.
The emperor, with frequency, 2600
received advisors, and they tried
to urge Alis to take a bride,
persisted at it without rest,
dwelt on it every day, and pressed
until they wore down his resistance.
He broke his pledge at their insistence,
agreed to what they had in mind,
but stressed that she must be refined,
wise, charming, beautiful, and noble,
this lady of Constantinople. 2610
Thus, his advisers let him know
they wanted to prepare to go
to German lands and to implore
the daughter of the emperor,
their preference as his bride-to-be.
The emperor of Germany
was very rich and powerful.
His daughter was so beautiful
that Christendom did not possess

[77]

2620 a rival with her loveliness.
Full leave the emperor bestowed,
whereon the lords took to the road
like well-outfitted personages.
The nobles rode their daily stages
to Regensburg, where they were brought
before the emperor and sought
the elder daughter of his house
as Emperor Alis's spouse.
The German emperor, content,
2630 gave his imperial consent.
His honor was not less the least,
and his prestige was not decreased.
His daughter's hand he would confer,
but warned that he had promised her
first to the duke of Saxony;
if she went with their company,
the duke would cause her harm or shame
unless the Grecian emperor came
and brought an army to attack
2640 the duke as they went riding back.
The German emperor replied
with such a message of the bride.
The lords took leave and came once more
before the Grecian emperor,
and this rejoinder they retold.
The emperor chose his most bold,
best-proven knights to do this feat.
His nephew was of this elite,
to whom he'd vowed to take no wife
2650 for the duration of his life,
a vow the emperor'd disown,
if only he could reach Cologne.*
The emperor Alis one day
rode out from Greece and went away

to Germany, which he approached.
However faulted or reproached,
he meant to marry nonetheless,
although his honor would be less.
He reached Cologne without a rest,
where, at the emperor's request, 2660
a German feast was being held,
and by the crowd the town was swelled.
The Greeks had finally reached Cologne,
by many Greeks and Germans grown;
some sixty thousand who came down
were forced to lodge outside the town.
A huge assembly had amassed.
The joyousness expressed was vast
by these two emperors, a pair
well pleased to see each other there. 2670
The palace hall was very long
and held the lords' assembly throng.
The emperor, when all were placed,
sent for his daughter in due haste.
The maid did not delay at all;
she promptly entered the great hall,
so beautiful, well formed of person,
that she seemed made by God in person
to win men's marveling regard
and to this end He labored hard. 2680
God, who made her, was disinclined
to give the words to humankind
to tell her beauty to the full,
for she was still more beautiful.
Fenice* was this fair maiden's name,
and hardly chosen without aim,
for as the phoenix is more fair
than other birds, so very rare
there's only one at any time,

2690 I think Fenice was as sublime;
her beauty peerless, lyrical,
a marvel and a miracle,
and Nature never could create
a replica or duplicate.
Her arms or body, hands or head
excelled what words I could have said,
so no description will I give.
Had I a thousand years to live
and every day my wits grew double,
2700 I still would have no end of trouble
in telling all of her that's true.
If I so undertook to do,
employing all my wit and skill,
my efforts would amount to nil,
and all my pains would be a waste.
The maiden made her way in haste;
she reached the great hall, entered there,
her head uncovered, her face bare;
her beauty, luminous and bright,
2710 lit up the hall with shining light,
more than four garnets, cut carbuncle.
Before the emperor, his uncle,
without a mantle, stood Cligès.
The day was touched by cloudiness,
but both were handsome to be seen,
so fair the beauty shared between
the maid and him cast forth a ray
that lit the great hall in the way
the sun would cast a very bright
2720 and reddish golden beam of light.
To do a portrait of Cligès,
I shall describe his handsomeness;
the passage will be brief, in truth.
Cligès was in the flower of youth,

for he had almost reached fifteen
and was as handsome in his mien
as that Narcissus* by the spring
beneath the elm tree, mirroring
himself, so loving his reflection,
they say, he perished of dejection   2730
from failure at possessing it.
He had great looks and little wit.
Cligès's sense was far more vast,
as copper is by gold surpassed,
far more good sense than I have told.
His head of hair resembled gold.
His face was like a fresh new rose.
He had a handsome mouth, straight nose,
and Nature's best work was his stature.
Good features that she tends to scatter   2740
in separate persons now all came
together in his single frame.
So generous Nature brooked no lack;
combining all within one pack,
she lavished it upon the lad.
Thus was Cligès, who in him had
sense, looks, strength, generosity.
In swordsmanship and archery
Cligès was skillful and knew more,
and more of bird and canine lore,   2750
than Tristan, nephew of King Mark.*
Cligès had wood as well as bark.
Cligès was lacking nothing good.
Before his uncle's seat he stood,
so handsome those stared at his place
to whom he was an unknown face.
As eager interest was displayed
by those who did not know the maid,
so all looked at her, marveling.

2760 Cligès, from love, kept swiveling
his eyes toward her, his glances fleet,
then turned them back to be discreet,
so none could think his wits astray
when he gazed toward her or away.
Admiring, he did not regard
how she from love, not from regard,
repaid him his admiring look.
She lent him her eyes; his she took.
She thought it profitable trade,
2770 and this exchange would strike the maid
as greater profit had she known
the least about him, save alone
he seemed a handsome youth to scan.
If ever she should see a man
and fall in love since he was fair,
she should not give her heart elsewhere.
Her eyes and heart she did impart
to him; he promised her his heart.
He promised it? Gave it outright!
2780 Gave? No, I lie, that is not right.
No one can give his heart away.
Let me rephrase what I shall say,
for I shall not be like somebody
who says "two hearts joined in one body."
A farfetched statement altogether:
one body with two hearts together;
and, even if they joined as one,
it seems unreal it could be done.
Attend, and you shall hear outright:
2790 I'll tell you how two hearts unite
and yet not actually connect.
Their union only has effect
insofar as the will* of each
can come within the other's reach.

They're one in will and in desire,
and to one thing they both aspire.
Since they both will one thing this way,
some people have been known to say
that each has both hearts in such cases,
but one heart can't be in two places.   2800
Their will can be one, theirs alone,
but each one's heart must be his own.
So just as many men, diverse,
can chant and sing in song and verse
together and in unison,
by this heartfelt comparison
I prove one body can't have two.
Know this is absolutely true.
Hearts are not how one penetrates
the things the other loves or hates;   2810
as voices joined to sing one note
cannot seem from one single throat
or all sound like the solo's part,
one body can have but one heart.
Upon this point I shall not dwell;
I have another tale to tell,
of greater urgency to stress,
about the maiden and Cligès.

THE COLOGNE TOURNAMENT

THE duke of Saxony, by plan,
had sent a very youthful man,   2820
one of his nephews, to Cologne,
who, to the emperor, made known
the duke his uncle said no use
to hope he'd grant a peace or truce
until his daughter was sent there.

Let anyone proceed with care
who thought to take the duke's intended.
He'd find the highway well defended,
not any clear or empty space,
2830   unless he'd yield her to his grace.
The youth spoke well, his attitude
was not contemptuous or rude,
but found all willing to ignore
his message, knight or emperor.
When, from disdain, they all kept silence,
he left the court out of defiance,
in passing challenging Cligès
from juvenile rambunctiousness.
To start the tourney, both sides mounted.
2840   Their number on each side amounted
to some three hundred for this game,
so that their numbers were the same.
No men or women stayed at all;
they cleared and emptied out the hall.
No knight or maiden passed the time,
for all of them began to climb
to balconies and to high places,
to battlements and window cases,
so they could view and watch the sight
2850   of those who were to joust and fight.
The maiden even went above,
for she was conquered now by Love
and in submission to his will.
She sat beside a window sill,
where she remained delightedly,
for from the window she could see
the one who stole away her heart,
with which she would not have him part.
No lover but him would she claim
2860   but did not even know his name,

identity, or line, or sire,
nor could she properly inquire.
She longed to hear someone employ
some words to fill her heart with joy.
She viewed the windowed tourney field,
where gold was gleaming on each shield
and those who bore the shields about
their necks while sporting in each bout.
The maiden's gazes and her thought
were elsewhere than on where they fought.   2870
She only strove to watch Cligès.
Her eyes pursued him in the press
and followed him wherever he went,
and he strove, in the tournament,
to joust for her conspicuously,
so she would only hear him be
held brave and skilled in estimate,
for it was quite appropriate
if she admired his valorousness.
At the duke's nephew rode Cligès.   2880
The nephew had a winning streak
of breaking lance and toppling Greek.
Annoyed by such fine horsemanship,
braced in his stirrups, with firm grip,
Cligès rode toward him at top speed
and knocked the young man off his steed.
The force left empty saddlebows;
to great commotion he arose.
The youth remounted, and he came
intending to avenge his shame.   2890
Some who seek vengeance when abased,
and have the chance, are worse disgraced.
The youth raced on in his advance.
Cligès replied with lowered lance,
attacked the youth with might and main,

and hurled him to the ground again.
The nephew's shame was now redoubled;
his people all were greatly troubled.
They knew that he would not be sent
2900 with honors from this tournament.
Not one could prove of such repute,
who had Cligès in hot pursuit,
that he could hope to keep his seat.
So, when they saw their men defeat
the Saxons on the field that day
and send them off in disarray,
the Greeks and Germans felt delight
and chased the Saxons out of spite,
until a river crossed their path
2910 where many Saxons took a bath.
Cligès tossed deepest in the ford
the nephew of the ducal lord,
and with him many of the rest,
who took to flight, ashamed, distressed,
downcast, and saddened, and concerned.
Then, joyfully, Cligès returned.
Both sides agreed he won the day.
He went straight to an entryway,
a doorway near the lodgings where
2920 the maiden was, and paid her fare;
she charged a toll of one sweet look
which, as his eyes met hers, she took.
Thus each was overcome by each.
Each German capable of speech,
come from the north or from the south,
had questions like these in his mouth:
"This youth in whom great beauty flowers,
Lord, who is he, and with what powers?
How did he happen, and so fast,
2930 to win the glory he amassed?"

[86]

The people asked repeatedly:
"Who is this child, who can he be?"
till everybody knew the truth,
throughout the city, of this youth,
his own name, and his father's name,
the pledge he had a right to claim:
the grant the emperor once said.
The talk of it grew so widespread
the maiden even heard it voiced,
and in her heart she well rejoiced.   2940
She can't say Love has shown disdain
and has no reason to complain:
Love made her love the handsomest,
the bravest, and the courtliest
of men to be found anywhere,
yet one for whom she could not care
was being forced on her instead.
She was distressed, dispirited,
and if advice could be acquired
about the man whom she desired,   2950
she did not know to whom to turn.
She lay awake in deep concern.

THESSALA'S SORCERY

AT these two problems, her distress
made her turn pale and colorless.
Her loss of color when upset
reflected her intense regret
she was not having things her way.
She was much less involved in play,
laughed less, did less that she enjoyed,
but hid how much she was annoyed   2960
and made denials that were strong

if someone asked her what was wrong.
Her governess, who was well versed
in necromancy and had nursed
the maiden in her infancy,
was Thessala of Thessaly,*
a place with deviltries so fraught
they are established and are taught.
The women born in Thessaly
2970   work charm and spell and sorcery.
When Thessala saw the maid constrained
by Love looked pallid, wan, and drained,
she asked her: "Dear sweet maiden, tell,
say if you fell beneath a spell
that makes your countenance so pale?
I wonder greatly why you ail,
and since you know, do make it plain
just where this ailment's caused most pain.
If anyone can cure your ills,
2980   rely on me, with all my skills.
Good health for you I can procure;
for dropsy I can work a cure,
and quinsy, asthma, and the gout.
I even know so much about
the state of urine and the pulse
for doctor you need no one else.
If I dare mention such enhancements,
I know some spells and some enchantments
that are well proven, real, and true,
2990   more than Medea ever knew.
Yet I have never said one word
before to you of what you've heard,
although I brought you up with care.
Do not blame me; I would not air
my lore except, with certainty,
I have perceived some malady

[88]

is overwhelming your resistance,
so you have need of my assistance.
It would be wiser if you told
before it gets a firmer hold   3000
and then extends its grip at large.
The emperor made you my charge
as your protector and your guard,
and I have worked so very hard
that I have kept you sound and hale.
My efforts all are doomed to fail
if I don't cure this malady.
Take good care, do not keep from me
an illness or what else you feel."
The maiden did not dare reveal   3010
her full desire for, once disclosed,
she greatly feared that, if exposed,
she would be cautioned or be blamed.
But now that Thessala proclaimed
her skill and sought to emphasize
and boast to her that she was wise
about enchantment, skill, and potion,
she'd tell the cause of her emotion,
but first, before the maid explained
what made her face so pale and drained,   3020
she made her pledge not to forbid
her will and always keep it hid.
"I don't believe, nurse, truthfully,
that I feel any malady,
but I believe I shall in time.
The thought makes pain begin to climb,
and I feel terrible distress.
What's sickness and what's healthiness?
Unless one feels them both, who knows?
Mine differs from all other woes.   3030
Were I to tell the truth again,

[89]

it pleases me yet causes pain,
for I delight in my unease,
and if a malady can please,
then my affliction suits my will,
whereas good health now suits me ill.
I don't know why I seek recourse.
I feel no pain from any source
unless I willed it and it came;
3040 although my will may merit blame,
I'm so at ease in my volition
it is a painful, sweet condition.
The joys that in my illness dwell
make it feel sweet to feel unwell.
Nurse Thessala, would you admit
this illness is a hypocrite
to cause me pain while seeming sweet?
I wish I knew without deceit
if or if not it seems to be
3050 an illness or a malady.
Nurse, tell its name or nomenclature,
the course it follows, and its nature,
but know I have no wish to heal.
I cherish all the pain I feel."
Then Thessala, who was most wise
in Love, his every way and guise,
could recognize from what she said
that Love had made her lose her head.
Because she called her suffering sweet,
3060 she was in love, without deceit.
All other sicknesses are bitter
save lovesickness, the one misfitter;
that ailment turns its bitterness
to sweetness and to gentleness
and often flips them back in place.
But Thessala, who knew the case,

replied, "Your fears are not in order;
and with respect to your disorder
both name and nature I'll reveal.
It seems you've said the pain you feel   3070
appears like joy and healthiness.
By nature so is lovesickness,
and from it come both joy and pain.
You are in love, I ascertain;
moreover, I can prove the thing.
In sweetness is no suffering
except in love and only there.
One point all other ailments share:
they're always awful and horrific,
but love is sweet, calm, and pacific.   3080
You are in love, I've certain proof,
which I don't think deserves reproof,
but I shall think you are remiss
if foolishness or cowardice
makes you conceal your heart from me."
"Why, lady, you speak pointlessly
unless I have no apprehension
that you might ever chance to mention
my feelings to a living soul."
"Be sure the winds will tell the whole   3090
before I mention your condition,
unless you give me your permission.
I pledge, moreover, and attest
I will promote your interest,
so you may certainly be sure
that what you will I shall procure."
"Nurse, you could cure my malady,
except the emperor weds me.
How sad and angry I do feel
because the man with such appeal   3100
is nephew to the man I'll wed.

If he enjoys me in his bed,
my joy is lost in that respect,
and I shall have none to expect.
I should prefer to be dismembered
than have our mutual love remembered
like that of Tristan and Isolde,
of whom much foolishness is told
that's shamefully recalled and said.*
3110   As for the life Isolde had led,
it never could be to my taste
because, in her, love was abased.
With one her whole heart was obsessed;
by two her body was possessed.
She lived this way her whole life through
and never once refused the two.
So this love was not reasonable,
but my love always will be stable,
and I shall never try to part
3120   and split my body from my heart.
My body won't be ill reputed,
to two shareholders prostituted.
Who has the heart shall have the body;
none else, excluding everybody.
How is my body to be tendered
to him to whom my heart surrendered?
My father's giving me away
to one whom I dare not gainsay.
When of my body he is lord
3130   and does things I would not accord,
it would be wrong of me to plan
to welcome any other man.
The emperor can't wed unless
he breaks his promise to Cligès,
to whom the empire will belong
at death, unless he does him wrong.

If you prevent, by skills and art,
the man from having any part
of me to whom I'm given, plighted,
your service will make me delighted.   3140
Nurse, you must make your effort now.
The emperor must keep the vow
he made before Cligès's sire.
The terms his father set require
no marriage for the emperor.
He will soon break the word he swore
by joining me in weddedness.
So much do I esteem Cligès
I could be buried* far more willing
than cause Cligès to lose a shilling   3150
of heritance he should adorn.
So let no child of mine be born
to disinherit him, not ever.
Now, nurse, do labor and endeavor;
I'll be forever in your debt."
The nurse was willing to abet
the maiden's wishes and emotions
and said she'd brew so many potions
and conjure up such spells and charms
she need not fear the emperor's arms   3160
as soon as he had drunk the drink   a
that she would give to him to drink.   b
Although in bed they'd lie together,   3161
the couple would not lie together.
She'd feel as safe as she would do
were there a wall between the two,
although she must remain composed
if he took pleasure while he dozed.
When fast asleep, this slumberer
would have his fill of joy with her
and, waking, would believe completely

[93]

3170   he had enjoyed her very sweetly
and would think none of his confusion
a dream, a lie, or an illusion.
He'd always make this same mistake
and, sleeping, think himself awake.

ALIS'S WEDDING

THE maid was gratified and praised
this kindly service; her nurse raised
her hopes by what she pledged to do
and what she promised would ensue,
however long she might postpone
3180   the joy she hoped would be her own.
Cligès would never take it wrong
were he to learn her love was strong,
and she intended to employ
a means of abstinence from joy
(preserving her virginity
and saving him his legacy).
He'd not be totally unkind
if he by nature was refined
and all he was supposed to be.
3190   She trusted her nurse utterly
and placed in her complete reliance.
Each pledged the other full affiance
to hold their secret conference
henceforth in total confidence.
Discussion ended as they swore.
When morning came, the emperor
sent for his daughter, and she joined
the company as he enjoined.
Now what, when all is said and done?
3200   So these two emperors, as one,

had their affair accelerated
and had the marriage celebrated.
In the great hall rejoicing reigned,
but I don't wish to be detained
by telling all about the feast,
for Thessala had never ceased
to make her potions, blend, and brew,
so I shall turn to her anew.
First Thessala ground her infusion,
then added spices in profusion   3210
to smooth it out and make it sweet.
She blended them and mixed and beat
and strained the brew to clarity
with no taste of acridity.
The brew was sweet to smell and taste
from spices with which it was laced,
and when her potion was all done,
the full course of the day had run.
The wedding supper had been made,
the tables placed, the linens laid.   3220
Of supper I shall say no more.
But Thessala was looking for
some bearer or expedient
by which her message could be sent.
At table, all the guests were met
by courses, over ten were set.
She saw it was Cligès who served
his uncle; Thessala observed:
"What wasted service to advance
thereby his disinheritance."   3230
To watch him serve left her distraught,
and then she had the pleasant thought
to have the drink served by a waiter
with joyous profit from it later,
so it was for Cligès she sent.

[95]

At once to Thessala he went
and asked her what she might intend.
She told him: "At this dinner, friend,
I want to treat the emperor.
3240   I have a drink he will adore.
Let me be perfectly forthright
that, by Saint Richier, tonight
I don't want him to drink a wine
or beverage apart from mine.
I think he'll love it, for he should;
he's never tasted one as good
or any drink as high in cost.
I would not have my warning lost:
let no one other drink of it,
3250   for there is just a little bit.
Then, I advise you to disclaim
all knowledge of from where it came,
except you chanced upon its presence
among the other wedding presents
and tasted it and were enticed
because it smelled so nicely spiced
and, seeing it so clear and fine,
within his cup you poured the wine.
Should he ask where it was procured,
3260   he will indeed be reassured.
You must not let what I have said
arouse suspicions that are dread.
The drink is healthy, clear, and nice,
and full of good, delicious spice.
I think that at some time, Cligès,
the drink will bring you happiness."
Cligès heard he would benefit;
he took the potion, carried it,
and poured it in a crystal cup,
3270   not knowing any harm was up,

and placed it by the emperor.
The emperor, who set great store
by him and thought his nephew true,
drank long and deeply of this brew.
He felt its potent forces start
descending from his head to heart
and rise from heart to head and seize
and move through his extremities
and leave him unimpaired throughout.
He had so long a drinking bout   3280
with this brew with its fine bouquet
when people took the cloths away,
he'd slumber nights in drunken fit
and never would be free of it.
This potion he had drunk so deep
made him feel wakeful while asleep.
The emperor's tricked at his wedding.
Came bishops, abbots to the bedding,
which they signed with the cross and blessed.
When came the time to go and rest,   3290
the emperor did as was right
and lay beside his wife that night.
Did as was right? I've lied in this;
he gave her no caress or kiss;
they lay together in one bed.
The maiden trembled, filled with dread
and with great doubts and great chagrin
the brew might not be genuine.
The potion had him so enchanted
he never would have what he wanted   3300
of her or others, save in sleep,
and then such sporting would he keep
as someone in a dream could feel
and would believe his dreaming real.
But nonetheless she feared the worst

[97]

and moved away from him at first,
but found she could not be approached.
Immediately sound sleep encroached.
He dreamed he was awake, a hoax,
3310   and took great pains and care to coax
the maid, resisting as she could,
protective of her maidenhood,
which she endeavored to defend.
He begged and called her his sweet friend,
whom very tenderly he sought,
yet he held nothing save in thought.
This nothing caused him ease and bliss.
With nothing to embrace and kiss,
he talked to nothing, nothing held,
3320   hugged nothing, nothingness beheld.
He wrestled nothing, strove with nil.
The potion had been brewed with skill.
Great were his effort and his pain,
and all for nothing and in vain,
for he believed he held the fort,
had captured it from his consort,
was spent, and needed some repose.
Thus he believed; thus he'll suppose.
I've told you once for all, he'll savor
3330   no other joy, so his behavior
must be forever and a day,
if he can take the maid away.
Before she's safely home, I sense
he faces great impediments.
The emperor came from his bridal;
the Saxon duke had not been idle
to whom she had been given first.
He brought an army and dispersed
more men to fortify the borders;
3340   his spies at court were at his orders.

These spies informed him every day
how long the emperor would stay,
all preparations, each concern,
the time his party would return,
and where their routes and passes lay.
The emperor did not delay
for, once his wedding day had flown,
he set off blithely from Cologne.
The emperor of Germany
came with substantial company;   3350
the Saxon duke was at the head
of forces that he held in dread.

FENICE'S ABDUCTION AND RETURN

TO Regensburg both emperors
pressed on without a halt or pause.
Beside the Danube's bank their band
camped overnight in meadow land.
Where the Black Forest circumvents
some fields, the Greeks were in their tents.
The Saxons, keeping watch, saw fit
to set their campsite opposite.   3360
The ducal nephew, posted guard,
was keeping watch with close regard
to what advantage he could manage
to harm the Greeks and do them damage.
This youth was at his guard post when
he saw Cligès and four young men
ride out disporting in the fields.
They bore their lances and their shields
so they could joust and have some fun.
The nephew, if it could be done,   3370
would hurt and harm them in a bout.

[99]

With two companions he rode out,
and they concealed themselves and stood
within a valley by the wood;
the Greeks did not observe them rally
until they came out of the valley.
The ducal nephew charged and hit
Cligès and wounded him a bit,
a minor wound above the spine.
3380 Cligès bent over to incline
and make the lance the young man raised
pass over him and leave him grazed.
But when Cligès could feel the scratch,
he charged the youth who fought this match
and struck so hard in his advance
that through his frame he thrust his lance
and slew the nephew in this fight.
Then all the Saxons took to flight.
They held Cligès in so much dread
3390 that through the forest bounds they fled.
Cligès, not realizing the trap,
went boldly risking great mishap,
with no companions at his back.
Cligès pursued the Saxons back
to their own army, so he fared
toward where the ducal force prepared
for their assault and Grecian raid.
He chased the youths back with no aid.
The young men in despair deplored
3400 the fact that they had lost their lord,
so they came weeping on a run
to tell the duke the damage done
to his own nephew, much distressed.
The duke considered it no jest.
By God and all His saints he swore
throughout his lifetime nevermore

would he rejoice, his fortunes thrive,
and know the man was still alive
who had just slain his nephew dead.
The man who brought the slayer's head   3410
he would consider his great friend
for all the comfort he would lend.
One knight who was a braggart sniffed
he'd make Cligès's head his gift,
if that young man would wait that long.
Cligès gave chase and came headlong
at length among the Saxon host.
The braggart knight who made the boast
he'd take Cligès's head away
beheld him and did not delay.   3420
Cligès turned back to gain some space
because this knight was giving chase.
When he went dashing back to seek
his own companions, not one Greek
was to be found in evidence,
for they had gone back to their tents
where their adventure they recounted.
Together Greeks and Germans mounted;
the emperor wished them combined.
Throughout the army, as assigned,   3430
the barons armed and leapt to horse.
The Saxon spurred along his course
to find Cligès, a man he chased
completely armed, with helmet laced.
Cligès, who saw him come alone
and never wanted to be known
for cowardice or lack of nerve,
abused him verbally with verve.
The knight, who wanted to annoy,
first stupidly called him a boy,   3440
unable to conceal his views.

He said: "Boy, here you'll pay your dues
for my own lord, whom you left dead.
If I don't carry off your head,
I'm worth less than a phony bezant.*
I'll give it to the duke for present.
No other price will I arrange.
You for his nephew I'll exchange,
and he will profit by the trade."
3450   Cligès heard out this crude tirade;
the knight spoke like a foolish lout.
Cligès responded, "Sir, look out,
I challenge you; you shall not cleave
and take my head without my leave."
They went for one another's guard.
The Saxon missed; Cligès struck hard,
so that the knight and his war horse
fell in a heap upon the course.
The horse fell backward, a hard toss
3460   that broke his rider's leg across.
Cligès dismounted at the scene
and stood on grasses growing green,
disarmed the Saxon knight, rearmed
with armor of the knight disarmed,
cut off his head, and used the blade
the knight owned for the blow he laid.
Cligès stuck on a lance's tip
the head removed by swordsmanship.
In combat, if he met the duke,
3470   he'd serve it to him in rebuke
to whom the Saxon vowed instead
he would present Cligès's head.
He donned the Saxon's helm, concealed
his head, and seized the second shield,
not his, that of the Saxon knight
who had come out to him to fight.

He did that first and in due course
remounted on the Saxon horse
while letting his own charger stray,
to cause the Greeks intense dismay.   3480
He saw some hundred banners fixed
above large, full-sized troops, which mixed   3482
the Greeks and Germans, who were merged.   a
Now the approach of battle verged;   b
the Greeks and Germans both were vicious,   3483
extremely cruel, and malicious.
Cligès saw them and by design
went racing toward the Saxon line.
His own troops failed to recognize
Cligès attired in Saxon guise.
His uncle was distressed the more
to see the head his lance tip bore,   3490
for he believed and thought with dread
it was his nephew's severed head.
No wonder at his fearfulness.
His army all pursued Cligès,
who wanted to begin the fray
and made them follow him this way
till he came in the Saxons' view.
His arms deceived the Saxons too,
for, as equipped, he meant to dupe
and to deceive the Saxon troop,   3500
so he rode up with lance at rest.
The Saxon duke and all the rest
exclaimed, "Our knight rejoins our band!
Upon the lance he has in hand
Cligès's head is stuck in place.
Behind, the Greeks are giving chase.
To horse to help him, everyone!"
The Saxons let their horses run.
Cligès spurred toward the Saxon field

[103]

3510 bent over low beneath his shield,
lance forward, head on iron part.
Although he had a Samson's heart,
he was not stronger in physique.
On both sides, Saxon, German, Greek,
Cligès's death was now believed.
The Saxons cheered, the others grieved,
and yet in time the truth would out.
Cligès was not still; with a shout
he sought a Saxon with a smash
3520 to center chest with lance of ash,
whereon the head was still impaled,
unhorsed the man whom he assailed,
then cried to German lords and Greek:
"Strike, lords! I am Cligès you seek!
Come on, brave knights, all bold and proud!
Do not let one of you be cowed!
We've won the first charge we have faced,
a meal no coward gets to taste!"
The emperor indeed rejoiced
3530 to hear the calls his nephew voiced
to make his army ride ahead,
which left him pleased and comforted.
The Saxon duke was much dismayed;
he realized he was betrayed
unless his was the greater force.
He made his men close up perforce.
The Greeks, close ranked to join the fray,
were not remaining far away.
They spurred and galloped on their ride.
3540 With lances leveled on each side,
they struck and suffered blow and thrust
as of necessity they must.
At first encounters, when they crashed,
the shields were pierced and lances smashed,

snapped girths, cut stirrups, saddles bare
that many mounts were left to wear
by those who lay about the site.
No matter how the rest might fight,
Cligès and duke began their bout,
and they both held their lances out   3550
and struck each other's shields so hard
their lances turned to bit and shard
and flew apart at their onslaught,
and they were sturdy and well wrought.
Cligès, in horsemanship first rate,
stayed in the saddle, sitting straight;
he kept his seat and was not shook.
The duke unwillingly forsook
his stirrups, and he lost his seat.
Cligès endeavored to defeat   3560
the duke and lead him off a prize,
a feat he could not realize.
The Saxons grouped around their lord
and rescued him at point of sword.
Cligès, unharmed by this dispute,
came off the battlefield with loot.
He carried off the duke's own charger,
as white as wool, whose worth was larger
than that of Rome's Octavian,
for it was an Arabian,   3570
which any lord would value thus.
The Greeks and Germans, rapturous
Cligès was on the Arab mount,
a horse they knew of such account,
had no suspicion of a trap
and were to suffer grave mishap
and loss when they were so deceived,
a trap they in no way perceived.
Now to the duke came an envoy,

3580 a spy who brought him greatest joy.
"None capable of self-defense
remains, sir, in the Grecian tents.
So you can have, believe my thought,
the emperor's own daughter caught,
and you can have the girl coerced
while you behold the Greeks immersed
in combat, skirmishes, and fights.
Give me a number of your knights
to whom your sweetheart I'll convey.
3590 By an old solitary way
so skillfully I'll lead them forth,
no German from the south or north
will see or meet our companies
until they reach her tent and seize
the maiden who is so exposed.
They will abduct her unopposed."
That idea made the duke content;
together with the spy he sent
one hundred seasoned knights and more.
3600 The spy led them so well, they tore
the girl away a prisoner.
They did not use much force with her;
she was an easy mark to find.
When once the tents were far behind,
they had twelve take the maid away.
The troop escorted a short way
the twelve who had the maid in tow,
then sought the duke to let him know
it had been a successful ruse.
3610 Then, with the Greeks he made a truce
to last until that night had sped,
since he had what he coveted.
The truce was offered and not spurned,
whereon the ducal men returned.

The Greeks delayed no more but went,
and each withdrew within his tent.
Cligès was at a lookout post
alone, unnoticed by the host.
He saw the twelve knights as they sped
on with the maiden whom they led,   3620
all galloping or at a run.
Cligès sought praise that was hard won
and sped toward them immediately.
They were not fleeing randomly,
his mind and heart told him the same.
The moment that he saw they came,
he followed, and they saw him race
and thought their own duke gave them chase.
The twelve said, for his benefit:
"Let's wait for him a little bit.   3630
To follow us our duke has flown
and left the army all alone."
So all believed of one accord.
All twelve knights wished to meet their lord,
each on his own in solitude.
A great vale's slope Cligès pursued
between two mountains. In their guise,
with banners hard to recognize,
Cligès did not know those whose fate
it was to come to him and wait   3640
until the first six had begun
to meet Cligès there one by one.
The rest stayed with the maid instead.
At walk or amble she was led,
both gentle paces to proceed.
Six spurred ahead at highest speed.
Along a vale these Saxons raced.
The one whose horse was fastest paced
left all behind to shout with glee:

[107]

3650 "God save you, duke of Saxony!
We have recovered your sweetheart.
Now with the Greeks she won't depart;
to you she soon will be returned."
When he had heard these words and learned
what news this man had come to bring,
it did not cause his heart to sing.
A wonder he was not insane.
No animal of some wild strain,
a leopard, tiger, lion crossed
3660 by seeing that its young were lost
was so enraged by such a sight,
so wrathful, or prepared to fight.
So was Cligès; he would not try
to live without her; better die
than not to have her back again.
Cligès was wrathful in his pain;
his rage made him grow bold indeed.
He pricked and spurred the Arab steed,
and at the painted shield he stabbed
3670 with so much force that, when he jabbed,
within his heart the Saxon felt
lance iron from that blow he dealt,
which made Cligès feel much assured.
He pricked his Arab steed and spurred
more than a measured acre's span
till he approached another man,
because they came in single file,
and he did not fear any while
he could joust singly with each one.
3680 He met them one by one, and none
could help the other one. The second
Cligès assailed, the knight who reckoned
he'd tell Cligès the maid was seized
and by his loss he would be pleased,

thus following the first knight's lead.
Cligès paid this next knight no heed,
ignored the words he tried to frame,
and thrust his lance into his frame.
He pulled out; blood sprang from the hole
and took away both speech and soul. 3690
He faced the third, behind this couple,
who thought that he would find him supple
and cheer him with what caused distress
and spurred his charger toward Cligès.
Before he spoke one word to fathom,
Cligès's lance was thrust a fathom
straight through his body, and the fourth
Cligès left senseless on the swarth,
stunned by the impact of his drive.
From four he went for number five. 3700
From five he went for number six,
and none withstood his fighting tricks.
He left them mute and taciturn.
With six no reason for concern,
he was less fearful of the rest,
who could more boldly be addressed.
When he was sure of six, he came
to make the rest a gift of shame,
a present with misfortune laden
for those who led away the maiden. 3710
He came on them and struck the way
a wolf will leap upon its prey
when it is famished, gaunt, and worn.
He thought himself most lucky born
to have occasion openly
to do bold feats of chivalry
before one so intoxicating.
He must succeed at liberating
the maid or die, and her distress

3720   brought her near dying for Cligès;
she did not know he was so near.
A strike that brought Cligès much cheer
with lance at rest he had begun:
he struck one Saxon knight, plus one,
so he got two on one same bound,
and threw both Saxons to the ground
and shattered his own lance of ash.
They were in anguish from their crash,
and neither knight could rise again

3730   to cause him injury or pain;
their bodies were too hurt and weak.
Four knights, all angered, went to seek
Cligès together; thus beset,
he was not shaken or upset
and kept his saddle underneath.
At once he drew forth from its sheath
his sword of steel, a sharpened blade.
To win the praises of the maid,
anticipating love's delight,

3740   he galloped at a Saxon knight
and with sharp sword a blow he sunk
that severed from the Saxon's trunk
his head and one half of his neck.
Of pity he showed not a speck.
Fenice, who watched him, could not guess
if he were or were not Cligès.
She wished he were and not a stranger,
and yet because he was in danger
she said she did not so intend.

3750   Thus on two counts she proved a friend:
she feared his death and wished him fame.
With his sharp sword Cligès took aim
at three knights, whose defense was fierce.
His shield their blows could crack and pierce;

to catch him was of no avail,
nor could they rend his coat of mail,
and nothing could withstand the blade
each time Cligès's blows were laid.
He cut them down, broke through nonstop,
and spun round faster than a top   3760
that's spun and driven by the whip.
His binding love and swordsmanship
made him aggressive as he warred.
He drove the Saxons very hard;
he killed and conquered to the last,
some slain, some wounded and aghast,
except he freed one of their band
with whom he battled hand to hand,
so that from him the duke would learn
his loss with sorrow and concern.   3770
Before that knight went on his way,   a
he urged Cligès to tell and say   b
his name and told the duke, his lord,   c
who learned of it with wrath untoward.   d
The duke, when told of his ill fate,   3771
was deeply saddened and irate.
Thereon Cligès took back Fenice,
by Love tormented without cease.
If he refuses to confess,
Love will cause him prolonged distress,
and her as well if she keeps still
about her pleasure and her will.
In privacy they could reveal
to one another how they feel,   3780
but they so fear rejection's darts
they dare not open up their hearts.
He feared refusal did he dare.
She would have laid her feelings bare,
except she feared to be refused,

[111]

and yet their thoughts could be perused
by one another through the eyes,
had either one made that surmise.
Their looks allow their eyes to speak;
3790   their mouths are cowardly and weak
and dare not speak in any guise
of love, in which they agonize.
No wonder she dares not begin,
because, since she is feminine,
she should be timid and demure.
Why does he tarry, so secure,
for her a valiant vanquisher
who's only cowardly with her?
Lord! Why is she his only fear,
3800   a maid so shy, still, and sincere?
It seems to me that I am seeing
the hounds before the hare a-fleeing,
the beaver hunted down by trout,
the lambkin shove the wolf about,
the dove upon the eagle's tracks,
the peasant spurn his mattock ax
by which he toils and makes his living,
the duck cause falcon grave misgiving,
gerfalcon fleeing heron's strike,
3810   the minnow chasing off the pike,
the stag a-hunting lion down;
things are reversed, turned upside down.*
But now I feel an obligation
to volunteer an explanation
about true lovers we observe,
and why they lack the sense and nerve
to tell their thinking, face to face,
when they have leisure, time, and place.
You who are wise concerning Love,
3820   the usages and customs of

whose court you hold in loyal awe,*
and never violate his law,
whatever outcome may befall,
say if there's anyone at all
who sees the loved one come in sight
and does not tremble or turn white?
I shall refute in argument
all those who counter what I meant.
Who does not tremble and turn pale
and feel his wits and memory fail,   3830
has sought, like one to thieving prone,
what rightfully is not his own.
A man-at-arms who is not nervous
should not be in his master's service.
Without respect he feels no fear,
nor does he hold his master dear.
A man-at-arms who does not feel
respect will try to cheat and steal
his lord's possessions and dissemble.
A man-at-arms should start to tremble   3840
when his lord calls for him or sends.
One who commits to Love intends
Love to be master and his lord.
He should recall it and accord
Love reverence, service, and support,
if he desires to join Love's court.
Without fear Love is incomplete,
a burning fire that casts no heat;
a day with no sunshiny hours;
a summer season with no flowers;   3850
a comb whose honey has been lost;
a wintertime without a frost;
a blank book and a moonless sky.*
That is the way I would descry
the man not fearful or appalled,

for by him Love goes unrecalled.
So fear a lover must discover,
yet he should only fear his lover
and be emboldened for her sake.

3860   Cligès committed no mistake
in feeling fear of his sweetheart,
but he would not have failed to start
to talk of love and ask for hers,
let her prove willing or averse,
were she not married to his uncle.
His wound abscessed to a carbuncle;
the suffering became more vicious
because he dared not speak his wishes.
So they returned to their own folk,

3870   and anything of which they spoke
was not worth paying any heed.
Each mounted on a sturdy steed,
and toward the army ranks they rushed,
where everyone by grief was crushed.
Throughout the army sorrow reigned;
the truth had not been ascertained.
Cligès was dead; their grief was strong,
and yet what they proclaimed was wrong.
The troops were grieving for Fenice;

3880   they thought they'd not win her release.
So, on account of her and him,
the army camp was very grim.
They won't be long but will arrange
for the scenario to change:
the army's grief to joy was turned
when to the camp the pair returned.
Returning joy made sorrow fleeting.
The army gathered for the meeting,
and everyone assembled there.

3890   The emperors went as a pair

to meet them with great joyfulness
when they were notified Cligès
had brought the maiden and was near.
Each one wished avidly to hear
Cligès tell how he went to track
the empress down and won her back.
The ones who heard him when he told
began to marvel and extolled
his skill and courage when engaged.
Elsewhere the duke had grown enraged.   3900
He swore and stressed what should be done:
that if Cligès dared, one to one,
the two of them would fight a duel,
and what the duke proposed was cruel.
For if Cligès should win the day,
the emperor could go away
in safety with his maid in tow,
but were the duke to overthrow
Cligès, who'd caused him great abuse,
there was to be no peace or truce,   3910
and let each army do its best.
The duke, pursuing this request,
sent one of his interpreters
of Greek and German to converse
with those two emperors and say
the duke was eager for this fray.
The messenger began to speak
the German language and the Greek
so all knew what his message was;
it set the army troops abuzz.   3920
Please God, they answered in rebuke,
Cligès not battle with the duke,
and both the emperors disclosed
their terror of the duel proposed.
Cligès fell at the emperors' feet

to be permitted to compete
and asked them not to be concerned.
If he had pleased them, he had earned
this single combat in reward.

3930   If this prize they would not accord,
he never would stay one day more
beside his uncle emperor
for honor or his benefit.
He loved his nephew, as was fit,
and raised him by the hand and said:
"Dear nephew, I feel grief and dread
that after joy may come lament,
on battle you are so intent.
You've pleased me, I cannot deny,

3940   but it's distressing to comply:
in single combat you'll be flung,
when I consider you too young.
You are so proud of heart, I know,
that I would never dare say no
to anything you may demand,
for you have only to command,
and it will happen without fail.
If prayer were of the least avail,
you never would assume this task."

3950   "My lord, in vain you plead and ask,"
replied Cligès. "May God confound me
if I would take the world around me
while single combat I decline.
I don't see why you would incline
toward lengthy respite and delay."
The emperor allowed the fray
but wept for pity for the boy.
Cligès was shedding tears of joy.
There was no bid to gain more time.

3960   Before it was the hour of prime,

though tears were shed, it did occur
that by the ducal messenger
the duel with the duke was set
according to his terms and threat.
The duke's belief, firm and intense,
was that Cligès had no defense
against him and would never last,
and so he donned his armor fast.
Cligès was sure he could withstand
the fight with the defense he planned   3970
and thought and wished for nothing more.
He asked arms of the emperor
and wanted to be dubbed a knight.
His heart was eager for the fight,
desired, and coveted its charms.
The emperor gave him his arms
most graciously, and so he placed
his armor on himself in haste.
When he was armed from head to toe,
the emperor was in deep woe,   3980
but to his side the sword he clipped.
Cligès was totally equipped.
On a white Arab horse he swung.
Around his neck by straps he hung
a shield of tusk of elephant,
unbreakable, which did not flaunt
a paint to make the ivory bright.
His armor was completely white.
The trappings and the steed below
were whiter than the driven snow.   3990
Cligès and Saxon duke were mounted.
The word each sent to each recounted
that they agreed to meet midway.
Their people witnessing the fray
could not bear swords and lances both.

Each side would pledge and swear on oath
that none would be so bold to dare
to make a move in this affair
or do harm while the two should vie,
4000   no more than dare pluck out an eye.
They came together at the scene
of combat on these terms, each keen
to savor both the eulogy
and glory of the victory.
Before a single blow was hit,
the anguished empress had seen fit
to be escorted there, who pined
for young Cligès and, firm in mind,
resolved to die if he were killed.
4010   No one could help her, for she willed
she must be left to die with him;
her life without him seemed too grim.
When to the field all had repaired,
high- and low-ranking, young, gray-haired,
and guards were posted at their station,
the two clashed with determination.
Each broke his lance upon the course
before he tumbled from his horse,
for neither one could keep his seat,
4020   but both of them sprang to their feet
unhurt, rejoined without delay,
resumed their fight, and played a lay
upon their helmets as they met;
their helmets rang out a duet.
Both sides were shocked by their attack.
When from their helms the swords sprang back,
in every place on which blows came
it seemed the helmets were aflame
to those who watched the fighters vie;
4030   from helmets sparks began to fly

as smoking iron can disgorge
when drawn out of the blacksmith's forge
and on the anvil hammered out.
Both lords were lavish in their bout.
They dealt out blows in plenitude.
Each one repaid with promptitude
what he received, with greatest pleasure,
and neither cared to count or measure
but handed over unassessed
both principal and interest,   4040
unhesitant, without a break.
But that his first strike did not take
Cligès's life and cause his loss
had left the duke both hot and cross.
Determined he would overthrow
Cligès, he placed a mighty blow.
Beneath the stunning blow he dealt,
Cligès fell on one knee and knelt
at the duke's feet upon the field.
Had he been underneath the shield   4050
that took the blow that felled Cligès,
the emperor was shocked no less.
Let come whatever may betide,
Fenice became so horrified,
she cried out unrestrained, "Saint Mary!"
as loudly as her voice would carry.
That phrase was all that she could speak.
She lost her voice, then she grew weak.
She fainted, and she fell across,
her arms outstretched to make a cross,   4060
so that she slightly cut her face.
The nobles lifted her in place.
Upon her feet she was maintained
until her senses were regained.
But, notwithstanding how she seemed,

no one who saw her as she screamed
knew why she fell down in a faint.
No one found fault with her complaint,
but she won every man's acclaim,
4070   who thought she would have done the same
if he were in Cligès's place,
although that would not be the case.
But when Fenice was crying out,
Cligès could hear and had no doubt
about what she meant to impart.
Her voice restored his strength and heart.
Cligès leapt up at once, assuaged,
and came upon the duke enraged;
The Saxon duke became dismayed
4080   at the assault and strike he made
and found Cligès more truculent,
spry, hardy, and belligerent
than he had been, to ducal thought,
the first time that the pair had fought.
The duke, in fear of his assault,
replied, "God save me, I can't fault
your valor, young man, and your drive,
and were my nephew still alive,
whom I shall nevermore forget,
4090   I'd gladly let peace terms be set
and end the quarrel in your favor
and leave off this exhausting labor."
"When someone can't defend his right,
should he not forfeit it outright
or, forced to choose by an oppressor
between two evils, choose the lesser?
So, duke, what will your pleasure be?
For, when your nephew challenged me,
he was imprudent, and I aim
4100   to deal with you the very same,"

Cligès said, "if you will not cease
to fight and make a proper peace."
The duke, considering Cligès
seemed to increase in powerfulness,
thought that, before he was worn out,
he would do better in this bout
to give up midpoint on his wrath
and not pursue a parlous path
while at this impasse on his route.
The open truth and absolute   4110
he nonetheless did not make clear.
"Young man, you're noble and sincere
and bold of heart, I must concede,
but you are very young indeed,
so, if I kill or conquer you,
what compliments would be my due?
Of laurels I should have a dearth.
I'll see no lord or man of worth
to whom I ever could avow
that I had dueled with you now.   4120
It honors you; me it demeans,
but if you know what honor means,
then what an honor you can tout
that in the first and second bout
you could withstand me, then alone.
My inclination, on my own,
is to stop fighting and curtail
the duel and say you may prevail."
"Duke, that is unacceptable.
Ask peace out loud, perceptible   4130
to all those here whom we behold
so it shall not be heard or told
that you were kind enough to cede,
when it is mercy I concede.
If you would reach accord with me,

repeat it so all here will see."
The duke repeated he would cease;
they reached agreement and a peace.
However the accord was pledged,
4140   Cligès was praised and privileged.
The Greeks rejoiced on its behalf;
the Saxons had no cause to laugh.
All had seen clearly that, at length,
their lord was tired and losing strength,
and did not have the slightest doubts.
Had he fought better in the bouts,
this peace would never have been sworn,
for, if he could, he would have torn
Cligès's soul out of his frame.
4150   The duke returned in grief and shame
to Saxony, with cause to rue
that of his men not even two
thought other than that he had failed
and was a coward who had quailed.
To Saxony the Saxons went,
returning in embarrassment.
The Grecian force, without delay,
resumed Constantinople's way
with greatest joy and happiness.
4160   The way was open, for Cligès
had cleared it by his valiancy.
They were not in the company
lent by the German emperor.
He took leave of the Greeks once more,
and of his daughter, and Cligès,
and emperor, last to address,
and stayed behind in Germany.
The Grecian emperor with glee
rode on, exultant in his mind.

[122]

CLIGÈS, courageous and refined,   4170
  thought of his father's firm command
and thought he would approach, as planned,
his uncle emperor and pray
his leave to journey on his way
to Britain and start traveling
to see his uncle and the king,
the two he wished to know and meet.
Cligès proceeded to entreat
and ask the Grecian emperor
for leave to go to Britain's shore   4180
to see his uncle and his friends.
Though courteously he sought his ends,
his uncle said no straightaway,
when he had let him have his say
and heard out his request to move.
"Dear nephew, I do not approve.
You'd leave me to my great chagrin,
and from me you will never win
my willing leave and my consent.
I am most pleased and well content   4190
to make you my companion.
We'll rule my whole domain as one."
Cligès, displeased at being spurned
when to his uncle he had turned
with his request, was definite.
"Sir," he replied, "I am not fit.
My courage and my statesmanship
are not enough for partnership
with you or anyone who ruled.
I am too young and too unschooled.   4200
The empire I should not uphold.

Across the touchstone* we rub gold
to see if it is pure and fine.
The purpose of this wish of mine
is to be tested where it's known
that I can locate such a stone.
In Britain, if my valor's much,
there is a touchstone I can touch
and put myself to a true test
4210   whereby my skills can be assessed.
In Britain worthy men renowned
for honor and for skill abound.
Who would win honor ought to be
a member of their company.
As a good man's companion
there is much honor to be won.
Thus I request to take your leave,
and you may certainly believe
if you won't send me where I'm bent,
4220   I shall depart without consent,
unless you grant this boon of mine."
"Dear nephew, your request is fine.
Your manner makes it very clear
that I cannot retain you here
by my entreaties or by force.
May Heaven grant you in due course
the inclination to return.
Pleas, bans, and force, I can discern,
are not the way you'll be controlled.
4230   Abrim with silver and with gold
you'll have a bushel to transport,
and horses you may use for sport
I'll give to you of your own choice,"
words he had scarcely time to voice;
Cligès's thanks were prompt indeed.
Then all the emperor agreed

and meant to give Cligès as boon
were placed before him very soon.
He had his choice upon his trip
of assets and companionship,   4240
and for himself he went to choose
war horses of four different hues:
a sorrel, tawny, white, and black.
I let my story all but lack
a part that I should not omit.
He asked his sweetheart to permit
his leaving, came before Fenice,
commended her to Heaven's peace,
and knelt before her. Tears unquenched
fell from his eyes so that they drenched   4250
his tunic and its ermine trim,
and to the ground in front of him
he cast his eyes down in dismay
and did not dare look straight her way,
as if he'd wronged her, and the blame
made him appear consumed with shame.
Fenice was watching, timid, meek,
not knowing what he came to seek
or what concern had brought Cligès.
"Don't weep," she told him with some stress,   4260
"dear brother, friend, rise, I entreat.
Come here by me and take your seat
and tell me what it is you feel."
"What to tell, lady, or conceal?
I seek and ask you for permission,
because I must depart for Britain."
"Then tell me why you must depart,
before I give you leave to start."
"My father, on his dying day,
left word before he passed away   4270
I must not fail, for any reason,

to go to Britain for a season
as soon as I was made a knight.
There is no way I wish to slight
the last commandment of my sire.
From here to there I would not tire.*
From Greece to Britain's a long piece.
Were I to travel back to Greece,
from Constantinople, my abode,
4280 to Britain is a long, long road,
too long for me, I do believe,
but I may rightly take your leave,
since I am totally your own."
Many a tear and sigh and moan
at his departure did they hide.
No one whose eyes were open wide,
whose hearing was acute and keen,
could tell for certain at the scene
whether or not it might be true
4290 that there was love between the two.
Cligès, however apprehensive,
left promptly and departed pensive.
The emperor, in pensive mood,
remained with others prone to brood.
Fenice, most pensive, brooded most.
The thoughts with which she was engrossed
so swiftly multiplied their ranks
they had no bottom and no banks.
So pensively to Greece she came,
4300 where she had honor and acclaim
as lady and as empress, twined.
Cligès was on her heart and mind
wherever he traveled or sojourned.
She'd never wish her heart returned
unless he brought it back again;
he's dying as he has her slain

by lovesickness he also feels.
She will not heal unless he heals,
and he will never pay the price
unless she makes their payment twice.   4310
Her illness on her face was ranged,
for she was very pale and changed.
Where Nature delicately stained
her face, no pure, fresh tint remained.
She sighed and fell to weeping hard;
her empire held in scant regard
and those great honors she was due,
when once Cligès had said adieu.
His leave-taking Fenice detailed,
how his complexion changed and paled.   4320
In memory she could retrace
his tears, his countenance, and face,
and how he came to weep before her,
as if to worship and adore her
sincerely, humbly, on his knees.
It all was pleasure and sweet ease
to recollect in memory.
Thereafter, as a savory,
upon her tongue she put a spice
that, in exchange for Greece's price,   4330
the way that she interpreted
the meaning of the phrase he said,
she would not have it mean deceit.
She lived upon no other treat,
and nothing else could win her praise.
She was sustained by that one phrase
that caused her suffering to shrink.
She sought no other food or drink
except Cligès's last remark
on parting from her to embark: 4340
that he was totally her own.

[127]

That phrase was pleasing to intone;
it touched her tongue and then her heart.
It stayed in mouth and heart, apart,
so she could be more sure of pleasure.
She dared not lock away the treasure
with any other lock and key,
and no place of security
was safer than her heart's redoubt.
4350 She would not ever take it out;
she was so fearful thieves would steal,
a fear she had no cause to feel,
a flighty fear,* disprovable.
This asset was not movable
but rather like an edifice
no fire or flooding puts amiss
but ever, with disaster passed,
remains in one place standing fast.
She was uncertain and would try
4360 to learn on what she could rely
as her foundation and her base,
with several ways to build her case.
Alone she was deliberative:
affirmative and negative,
as she conducted this debate.*
"What did Cligès intend to state
by 'I am totally your own'
unless Love made him make it known?
What rights of mine be over him,
4370 who makes me lady over him?
Why does he think me of such worth?
He is a man of nobler birth;
in beauty he is handsomer.
This boon Love only could confer.
Now, I shall prove by my own case,
who can't escape Love any place,

unless he loved me, he'd decline
to make a statement he was mine,
as I would never make it known
I wholly am or was his own 4380
had Love not given me to him.
Cligès should not have said on whim
he was all mine or speak thereof
unless ensnared by bonds of Love.
If he loved not, he'd not fear me.
Love, who gave all me, his to be,
might give all him to me in turn.
And yet that phrase gives me concern,
for it is such a platitude
I may imagine being wooed. 4390
Some people who are newcomers
tell strangers, 'I am wholly yours
and so is all I have,' and chatter
far more than jaybirds when they flatter.
I'm still unsure, for it could be
he spoke that phrase to flatter me.
But I could see his color drain,
while tears fell he could not restrain.
My judgment is: the tears that rushed,
and air that was pathetic, crushed, 4400
do not arise from false deceit.
They were no trickery or cheat.
His eyes did not tell lies to me
when I beheld those tears fall free.
If I know anything thereof,
I saw therein the signs of love.
Yes, so much so, I thought and learned;
the memory of love returned,
and Love leaves me disconsolate.
For me it proved unfortunate. 4410
Unfortunate? Indeed, I say.

The man who stole my heart away
with flattering blandishments he said
has vanished, leaving me for dead.
My heart will not remain with me;
succumbing to his flattery,
far from its home it has gone hence
and spurns me and my residence.
The man who holds my heart secure
4420 has done me wrong, I feel quite sure.
He loves me not, so I have known,
who steals my heart and all I own.
Am I so sure? Why did he weep?
His tears weren't purposeless or cheap;
he had good reason why they fell,
and I am not responsible,
for people part with greatest woe
from others whom they love and know.
When he left someone whom he knew,
4430 he would have had good cause for rue;
I do not wonder that he wept.
Whoever got him to accept
advice to go and stay in Britain
struck to my heart and left me smitten.
Heart-stricken means to lose one's heart;
one suffers when it is one's part,
but I have not deserved such pain.
Alas, Cligès, why leave me slain
when I've done nothing to revile?
4440 Why have I put Cligès on trial,
for I do not have any reason,
nor would Cligès, in any season,
have left me, I have surely known,
not if his heart were like my own.
But like my own his cannot be.
Were my heart to join company

with his heart, it would not depart,
nor would his leave without my heart,
for after his heart mine would slip,
so close is their companionship.   4450
To tell the truth, our two hearts vary;
they are divergent and contrary.
Why so contrary and divergent?
His heart is lord and mine is servant.
The servant does, despite himself,
whatever his lord thinks right himself;
from other cares he must be turned.
I am concerned; he's unconcerned
about my service and my heart.
Unfair in size is each heart's part,   4460
which makes one heart the lord of two.
Why, all alone, can't my heart do
as much as his heart does for him,
their power equalized and trim?
My heart remains a prisoner,
unless his own heart starts to stir,
and should his heart remain or roam,
my heart's prepared to leave its home
to follow him wherever he goes.
Why can't our bodies be so close   4470
that I could remedy my lack
and somehow get my own heart back?
Get it back! Fool, you are remiss.
If I removed it from its bliss
in such a way, it might be slain.
I will not! Let my heart remain!
Let it remain there with its lord's
until compassion he accords.
There he's more apt to be observant
and to take pity on his servant,   4480
because they are in foreign lands.

If flattery it understands,
to which court servants must resort,
it will be rich when it leaves court.
Who would be in his lord's good grace
and on his right side take his place,
as use and custom have now spread,
should brush the feather from his head,
even when feathers there are none.*

4490　There's one bad point to what he's done:
for he smoothes down his outside parts,
but if within his heart of hearts
the lord is wicked, base, and low,
the courtier will not tell him so
but will attempt to make him see
in wisdom and in bravery
he's unsurpassed and has no peer;

4498　his lord will think he is sincere.
a　A man lacks insight who is buoyed
b　by praise of what he is devoid.
4499　The lord may be perverse by habit,
4500　cruel, wicked, timid as a rabbit,
demented, stingy, misinformed,
in body twisted and malformed,
in word and deed completely base,
a man will praise him to his face
and make a face behind his back
but in his hearing will not lack
for praise his lord can overhear
in a discussion with some peer.
If he thought him past range of voice,

4510　he'd not thus make his lord rejoice.
Now, if his lord decides to lie,
4512　in all he's willing to comply,
a　and what his lord as truth affirms
b　his tongue expansively confirms.

[132]

A man must serve with false pretense 4513
the courts and lords that he frequents.
My heart must do so in such case,
if it desires its lord's good grace;
it must be flattering and coax.
Yet highest praise would be no hoax,
because Cligès is such a knight,
so handsome, loyal, and upright 4520
my heart sincerely will approve.
In him there's nothing to improve.
I want my heart to serve Cligès.
The peasant tells the worthlessness
of one who serves a gentleman
and yet is not a better man."
Love, thus belaboring Fenice,
delighted her without surcease.

THE WALLINGFORD TOURNAMENT

CLIGÈS had gone across the sea
to Wallingford. Luxuriously 4530
he lived therein, at great expense,
his lodgings a fine residence.
He always thought about Fenice,
and not for one hour did he cease
to have her constantly in mind.
When at the place he lodged and dined
he had his people ask around,
and from their inquiries they found
from those who lived in the environs
King Arthur's court and lords and barons, 4540
the king himself, were all intent
to organize a tournament.
Upon the plain by Oxford, toward

[133]

the nearby town of Wallingford,
the tourney would be held and last
until four days had come and passed.
Meanwhile Cligès had time to spare
to get accoutrements to wear,
if anything were incomplete.
4550 Before the tournament would meet,
a full two weeks would pass and more.
At once he gave three squires this chore:
to go to London and to choose
new armor in three different hues,
the first one black in shade and sheen,
the second red, the third one green.
When they returned, they were to swath
each set of armor in new cloth
so that nobody whom they met
4560 would know the color of each set
of arms they bore to his abode.
At once the squires took to the road
to London, where the arms they sought
they found available and wrought.
Their errand speedily was run,
and their return trip was begun.
The squires, returning in short order,
displayed the armor in the order.
Cligès praised them for what they did
4570 and had the sets of armor hid
with those that, on the Danube's shore,
were given by the emperor
when he had dubbed Cligès a knight.
Should someone ask me now to cite
why he would hide the arms away,
I would not be prepared to say,
but later you will understand,
when all the barons of the land

who seek renown for valiant deeds
have gotten mounted on their steeds.   4580
On the proposed and chosen day
all barons gathered in array.
King Arthur, with a chosen few
of best men in his retinue,
regrouped near Oxford, but the horde
of knights regrouped near Wallingford.
Do you believe that I should spin
my story out and should begin
to give a lengthier account:
"This king was there; so was this count;   4590
this, this, and this one did attend"?*
When those lords gathered to contend,
a custom of that time occurred:
A knight of greatest merit spurred
between the ranks divided twain;
a member of King Arthur's train
prepared to fight the opening bout,
but not a knight would dare step out
to joust with one of such great skill,
and all remained completely still.   4600
Some people there began to say:
"Why is it that these knights delay?
Won't one break ranks to meet this knight?
Soon someone will begin to fight."
A view that many more dismissed.
"No, see what an antagonist
is sent against us from that side?
Let everyone be notified:
among the greatest four knights known
is that knight in the square alone."*   4610
"Who is he?" "See? That warrior
is the hotheaded Sagremore."
"It is?" "Indeed." Cligès heard tell

[135]

while he was mounted on Morel.
His arms were black in hue and type
like blackberries that are dead ripe.
His armor was entirely black.
He broke ranks, started to attack,
and spurred Morel to make him race.
4620 Then all who saw him giving chase
told one another, much impressed:
"This knight proceeds well, lance at rest.
In skillfulness he has excelled;
his weapons are correctly held;
the shield at neck is by the rule;
and yet he may be thought a fool,
for in this joust he has addressed
a man who is among the best
knights known in all this country's borne.
4630 But who is he? Where was he born?
Who knows him? Not I. I don't know,
4632 but he has not been caught in snow.
a   His armor is as black at least
b   as any cowl of monk or priest."
4633 Thus went the talk of everyone.
The two knights let their horses run,
delayed no longer, filled with heat
and eager for their jousting meet.
Cligès struck hard so that he pressed
a shield to arm and arm to chest.
Pinned by the blow Cligès had laid,
4640 down Sagremore had fallen, splayed.
a   Cligès approached him, as he ought,
b   and made him pledge that he was caught.
4641 He pledged himself a prisoner.
Thereon the tourney could occur,
and people entered it pell mell.
Cligès joined in the fray and swell

to seek encounters and to fight.
He felled and captured every knight
with whom he jousted or he vied
and won the honors on each side.
The bouts he held wherever he went
would interrupt the tournament. 4650
Those who went jousting with Cligès
were not devoid of stalwartness.
To face Cligès showed more élan
than to defeat another man,
and to be captured by Cligès
would win praise for courageousness
for him who'd dared attempt a bout.
Cligès acquired great praise throughout
the tournament and battlefield.
Then he departed, well concealed, 4660
to where he lodged, so none could chat
or speak with him of this or that.
Lest anybody try to track
the lodging where the arms were black,
within a room Cligès consigned them
so nobody would see or find them,
but ordered, at the door that faced
the street, green arms and armor placed
in view of all the passersby.
If anybody came to try 4670
to ask for him, he could not trace
or find Cligès's lodging place. 4672
There was no sign of any kind a
of that black knight they came to find. b
Cligès in town did thereby choose 4673
to hide himself by such a ruse.
His prisoners were forced to wend
their way through town from end to end,
inquiring after that black knight,

and no one knew his lodging site.
King Arthur sent his folk to town,
4680   where they went searching up and down.
All said: "We've not seen where he went
since we came from the tournament,
and don't know where he can be found."
Some twenty young men looked around,
sent by the king for what they did,
and yet Cligès kept so well hid,
of that black knight they found no sign.
King Arthur made the cross's sign
when he was told no one at all
4690   knew of his lodgings; great or small,
nobody had the least idea.
He might have been in Caesarea,
or in Toledo or in Crete.*
"Now my amazement is complete.
Perhaps it was a phantom come
among us to make knights succumb.
My word, I don't know what to say.
He's toppled many knights today;
These pledges, which the best knights spoke,
4700   within one year's time will be broke
if they can't find the black knight's door
or land or country, as they swore."
The king thus stated what he meant
and might well have kept reticent.
The barons talked into the night
of nothing else but that black knight.
Next day, back to their arms all pressed,
without a summons or request.
A warrior not faint of heart
4710   arrived to make the jousting start,
the knight called Lancelot of the Lake;*
the first encounter he would take.

Not one to let this challenge pass,
Cligès came up as green as grass
that grows in meadow or in mead,
upon a long-maned, tawny steed.
There was no one, longhaired or bald,
who did not watch him come, enthralled,
in green upon the tawny steed,
and people on each side agreed: 4720
"He's skilled and noble, every way,
more than the black knight yesterday,
in the same manner that the pine,
compared with hornbeam, is more fine,
and elder is surpassed by laurel.
The knight attired in black apparel
of yesterday remains unknown.
Today this knight will be made known.
Tell us, who knows this knight in green?"
Yet each believed he'd never seen   4730
or known this knight, who in all ways
was handsomer than yesterday's,
more so than Lancelot of the Lake.
Yes, make him wear a sack and make
Lancelot wear silver and gold,
he'd still be fairer to behold.
It was Cligès whom all preferred.
The two collided as they spurred
and rode as fast as they could go.
Cligès dealt Lancelot a blow   4740
on his gold, lion-painted shield,
unhorsed him on the battlefield,
and came to him to take his word.
Defenseless, Lancelot concurred
and pledged himself Cligès's man.
Whereon the tournament began
with uproar, noise, while lances cracked.

Therein Cligès was fully backed
by those who fought upon his side.
4750   With those fierce blows that he applied,
however strong, opponents found
they fell from chargers to the ground.
That day Cligès performed so well,
so many of his prisoners fell
he pleased his own side two times more,
and double from the day before
was the prestige Cligès acquired.
At vespertide Cligès retired;
back to his lodging place he sped,
4760   where he displayed his shield of red
and other trappings straightaway.
The armor he had worn that day
he ordered hidden for a spell;
Cligès's host concealed it well.
The knights he'd taken prisoner
searched long to find their vanquisher
that night, with no news of his ways.
Most folk in lodgings sang his praise.
The knights, who were both strong and spry,
4770   returned to arms next day to vie.
Then, from the ranks of Oxford town
emerged a knight of great renown:
one Perceval of Wales he proved,
and when Cligès saw how he moved
and learned he had a rightful claim
to Perceval of Wales for name,
he longed to meet him and to quarrel.
Upon a Spanish steed, a sorrel,
he left the ranks and came ahead
4780   with arms and armor that were red.
The spectators all simply gazed.
they never had been so amazed

[140]

and said they never had caught sight
of such a fine and handsome knight.
The two spurred forward straightaway
and did not tarry or delay.
Thus one knight and the other spurred
until great blows could be conferred
upon the shield with short thick lance,
which bent and bowed with their advance.   4790
As people watched, in sight of all,
Cligès struck out at Perceval,
so that he knocked him off his horse
and thereon took his pledge by force
he was a captive; his assent
required scant talk or argument.
When Perceval had pledged his word,
the tourney opening occurred.
All came together for their fight.
Cligès collided with no knight   4800
he failed to hurtle to the ground.
That day Cligès could not be found
outside the tourney for one hour.
All struck on him as on a tower.
They did not strike by threes or twos;
at that time that was not the use
or custom of the tourney field.
He made an anvil of his shield.
All forged and hammered till it split
and shattered from their pounding it,   4810
but all who struck him paid the cost
of stirrups and of saddle lost,
and only liars would have said
the knight who bore the shield of red
had not defeated everyone
when that day's tourneying was done.
The courtliest and the elite

[141]

were wishing for a chance to meet,
but would not get acquainted yet,
4820   for when he saw the sun had set,
in secrecy he left the field
and had them take off his red shield
and other gear in which he fought.
He had the arms and armor brought
he'd worn when he was made a knight,
which, with the charger, were in sight
outside the doorway on display.
4828   But people had begun to say,
a   once they could ponder and reflect,
b   that obviously they could detect
4829   the fact that all were overthrown
4830   and routed by one man alone,
though every day he would appear
with some new charger, arms, and gear
to make himself seem otherwise.
They penetrated his disguise
for the first time, and Sir Gawain,
who'd seen no jouster in his vein,
said that he wished that he could claim
acquaintanceship and learn his name.
He said he would be first next day
4840   when knights assembled for the fray.
He did not boast at all of it
because, when leveled lances hit,
the other knight, he did suppose,
would win at that exchange of blows.
But with the sword it well could be
Gawain would show his mastery;
he had no master at swordplay.
He would be put to test next day
against the knight who was a stranger,
4850   a daily horse- and armor-changer,

who changed his trappings for his jolts
and would in time achieve four molts,
were it his wont, when each day looms,
to cast away and don new plumes.
Thus Sir Gawain spoke out and mused.
Next morning came, and he perused
Cligès returning, lily white,
as he arranged the previous night;
shield straps in hand, he rode his course
on his fresh white Arabian horse.   4860
Thereon brave, glorious Gawain,
who scarcely paused upon the plain,
urged on his horse and spurred and pricked.
If an opponent could be picked,
he'd joust as well as he could do.
Upon the field there'll soon be two,
because Cligès was undeterred
once that this murmuring was heard:
"It is Gawain, and one to count
a splendid knight on foot or mount.   4870
No one would want to take him on."
Cligès heard that and he was gone.
He hurtled toward him in midfield.
Toward one another both knights wheeled
and came together in a charge,
much faster than a stag at large
that hears hounds baying after it.
The lances aimed at shields and hit.
Then at both handles, leather-wrapped,
the lances shattered, split, and snapped.   4880
They gave each other such hard blows
they fragmented their saddlebows
and snapped the breast strap and the girth.
As equals, both knights fell to earth,
and they drew out their naked swords.

The people grouped around the lords
to watch the swordplay in their brawl.
King Arthur came before them all
to separate them with a truce.
4890 But they inflicted great abuse:
bright mail was torn, the links were cracked,
the shields they bore were pierced and hacked,
their helms were broken piece by piece
before there would be talk of peace.
Once that the king had watched a bit,
the length of time that he saw fit,
with many other folk who deemed
the white knight was not less esteemed
for handling weapons in the fray
4900 than Sir Gawain in any way,
because they could not tell for sure
which would prove better, which prove poor,
which would defeat the other knight
if they could be allowed to fight
until their battle reached its end
(King Arthur, though, did not intend
to have more done than they had done),*
the king advanced and told each one,
to separate them: "Back you go!
4910 Don't dare to strike another blow!
Instead, be friends, and make a peace!
Gawain, dear nephew, please do cease.
A gentleman would be at fault,
if he continued an assault
with quarrel or hatred of no sort.
If that knight would attend my court
to please us and is not averse,
he surely would be none the worse.
Invite him, nephew." "Gladly, sire."
4920 Cligès agreed, with no desire

to turn him down or to dissent
once he could leave the tournament,
for that command his father willed
he now had totally fulfilled.
King Arthur's interest was not strong
in tourneys that were overlong,
so he announced it was disbanded;
the knights left, as the king commanded.
Cligès, in preparation, sent
for all of his accoutrement,   4930
since he was following the king.
He came to court, not tarrying,
but first he dressed with elegance,
his wardrobe in the style of France.
As soon as he arrived at court,
a crowd ran out of every sort
and welcomed him, without a pause,
with greatest joy and great applause.
There was no more they could have done.
He was called lord by everyone   4940
he'd captured at the tournament,
but he made no acknowledgment.
All were released from what they pledged,
he told them, if they still alleged
he was the one who'd brought them low.
"But he was you, how well we know,"
each one of them persisted yet.
"We are so pleased that we have met.
Esteem and love we should accord
and should address you as our lord.   4950
None of us equals you, not one.
Just as the stars are dimmed by sun,
so that their light does not appear
in skies with sunbeams shining clear,
the knightly deeds we used to tout

are dimmed until they are snuffed out,
compared with those that you have shown,
although our deeds were once well known
throughout the world and much acclaimed."
4960 Cligès, delighted and ashamed,
was at a loss for a reply.
Their praises all appeared too high,
their adulation out of place.
The blood came rising to his face.
With his confusion seen by all,
he was escorted to the hall
before the king for audience,
but all left off their compliments.
It was already time they dined.
4970 The servers who had been assigned
to set out tabletop on base
ran out to put them in their place
for dinner in the palace hall.
Some servers held out towels for all,
and some held water basins out
to people who would dine throughout.
All washed their hands and sat in place.
The king sat down Cligès in face
by taking him there by the hand;
4980 his status he would understand
and wished to get him to reveal.
There's no need to discuss the meal;
each course was plentiful and filling,
as if an ox cost but a shilling.
When all their courses were consumed,
the king broke silence and resumed:
"Now, friend, I wish to understand
why, on your entry to this land,
you did not deign come to my court?
4990 Did pride make you fail to report?

Why keep from us and be estranged?
Why were your arms and armor changed?
Tell me the name that you have borne
and of what people you were born."
Cligès said, "It won't be concealed."
Then he recounted and revealed
all answers that the king desired.
Once that the king had thus inquired
and heard Cligès's answers voiced,
the king embraced him and rejoiced.   5000
When Sir Gawain learned, greatly buoyed,
he hugged him, the most overjoyed.
The rest embraced with joyfulness.
All who spoke of him termed Cligès
most handsome and heroical.
Compared with the king's nephews all,
more love and honor he attained,
and with the king Cligès remained
until the summer came anew.
By then Cligès had traveled through   5010
all Britain, France, and Normandy.
His many feats of chivalry
ensured Cligès was put to test.

CLIGÈS RETURNS TO GREECE

BUT LOVE, whose wounds were manifest,
was no less forceful or assuaged.
His heart's will kept his thoughts engaged
upon one subject without cease;
he always thought about Fenice,
and she obsessed him, though remote.
The thought he must leave Britain smote.   5020
Too long deprived, he now aspired

[147]

to see the lady most desired
of all for whom desire has thrived
and would no longer be deprived.
His plans to leave for Greece were formed.
On leave-taking, he so informed
the king and Sir Gawain, in grief,
they could not stall, in my belief,
the day on which Cligès returned.

5030 He was in love and deeply yearned
for one he sought by land and sea
and hurried toward her eagerly.
How long the way he traveled rolled,
for he was eager to behold
the one who stole his heart away.
She would make fair return, fair pay,
fair compensation for her stealing;
she'd give him back her heart, cash dealing,
because her love was not the less.

5040 That was not certain to Cligès,
with no commitment or accord,
and by self-torture he was gored.
She put herself through equal pain,
tormented by her love and slain;
she had seen nothing with the power
to please or suit her since the hour
he left her sight, and, worse misgiving,
she did not know if he were living,
so in her heart great sorrow passed.

5050 Cligès was now approaching fast,
and he was lucky altogether
to have fair wind without foul weather,
so with great joyfulness and sport
near Constantinople he made port.
News reached the city and, inside,
the emperor was gratified,

the empress more, one-hundredfold;
let no one doubt, when it was told
Cligès, together with his band,
in their return to Greece, would land   5060
right at the port of Constantinople.
All those most highly born and noble
came to the port to meet the men.
The emperor went forward then,
the empress at his side, and pressed
well in advance of all the rest;
to hug Cligès the emperor rushed.
Fenice hailed him, and each one flushed
because the other one was there.
A wonder, when it felt so fair   5070
to stand so close and face to face,
that they did not kiss or embrace
with kisses Love would have exchanged;
such folly would have been deranged.
From all directions people ran,
on foot and horseback, all began
escorting him with joyfulness
on through the town; to see Cligès
was great delight to them and solace.
They went to the imperial palace.   5080
At this place there will be no word
of the rejoicing that occurred   5082
and service of his retinue,   a
but everybody strove to do   b
what he believed and thought was best   c
to make Cligès pleased and impressed.   d
Cligès's uncle handed down   5083
all he possessed except his crown
and wished Cligès would take his pleasure
of his own silver or his treasure
as he desired to use or hold.

[149]

Cligès did not want silver or gold,
with thoughts that he dared not disclose
5090   to her who cost him his repose.
He could have spoken undiscerned
had he not feared he would be spurned,
for no one wanted to intrude,
and at her side in solitude
he could watch her all day and sit;
no one thought any harm of it.

AVOWAL AND PLANS

LONG afterward, all on his own,
    Cligès came to the room alone
of one who was no enemy,
5100   that you may know with certainty.
The door was not shut in his face.
He sat, half leaning, by her place,
and to the sides the rest withdrew,
so no one sat next to those two
to overhear as they conversed.
Fenice began with Britain first,
because she wished to ascertain
the character of Sir Gawain,
if he were polished and refined.
5110   She raised what preyed upon her mind,
a subject that she feared to cover.
She asked him if he had a lover,
a maid or lady of that land.
Cligès gave her to understand
at once, not being reticent
about disclosing what he meant:
"My lady, there I was love-smitten,
but I loved nobody from Britain.

When I was on the British shore,
like bark without a wooden core,   5120
my body was without a heart.
Where it's been since I went apart
from Germany, I have no clue,
except my heart has followed you.
My heart was here, my body there.
I never really went elsewhere;
to Greece returned the heart I lack,
which is the reason I came back.
Yet it will not return to me.
I can't restore it personally;   5130
it would be more than I could stand.
Since your arrival in this land,
will you not tell how you have been?
Have you enjoyed yourself since then?
How pleasing are the land and folk?
In answer, all I should evoke
is whether you are pleased with Greece."
"Greece has not pleased me," said Fenice,
"but I begin to feel some measure
of joy and pleasure. Prayer or pleasure   5140
could not make me forego one bit.
I can't detach my heart from it
and will not use force, brute and stark.
There's nothing left of me but bark.
I live and breathe without a heart.
From Britain I have kept apart,
but my heart made a lengthy stay,
for good or ill I cannot say."
"But when your heart stayed there a while,
tell me when it went to that isle,   5150
and at what time and in what season,
provided that, with every reason,
to me or others you could tell.

Was it when I was there as well?"
"Yes, but you were quite unaware.
My heart was there when you were there,
and afterward it left with you."
"Good Lord, I never saw or knew.
Good Lord, why not? If I had known,
5160   your heart would not have been alone;
I would have kept it company."
"And have been comforting to me.
Friend, you should not have kept apart.
I'd have been gracious toward your heart,
if it had pleased to come around
to where it knew I would be found."
"It found you, lady, without guile."
"It found me? It was no exile,
for my heart also went to you."
5170   "My lady, if your words are true,
here with us are both hearts we own,
for mine is totally your own."
"And my own heart in you is set,
my friend, and so we are well met.
God save me, know with certainty
your uncle had no part of me.
He's never known me in his life
the way that Adam knew his wife.
He had no chance, which I forestalled,
5180   so 'lady' I am wrongly called.
But those by whom I'm so portrayed
are unaware I am a maid.
Your uncle, even, has no notion,
for he has drunk some sleeping potion
and thinks he's wakeful when he dreams
and sports with me, or so it seems,
as if within my arms he lay,
but I have kept him well away.

Yours is my heart, yours is my body,
and at no time will anybody,   5190
with my behavior as a sample,
learn villainy from my example.
For when my heart went in your frame,
it made my body yours to claim;
no share will any other keep.
Love for you made a wound so deep,
I thought that I would never heal.
What suffering you have made me feel.
If I love you and you love me,
a Tristan you will never be,   5200
nor I be named as an Isolde,
for such love would not be extolled
but intermixed with vice and blame.
You never will enjoy or claim
my body otherwise than now
unless you plan and think of how
to steal me from your uncle and
conceal me somewhere so well planned
that he cannot find me anew
or lay the blame on me or you   5210
or even know which way to turn.
This evening, ponder that concern.
Tomorrow, tell me what you find,
the best ideas that come to mind,
and I shall think it through likewise.
Tomorrow, after I arise,
come speak to me, and we'll explain
the thoughts that we then entertain,
and when our thoughts have been expressed,
we'll choose the plan we think is best."   5220
Cligès, who heard what she devised,
considered she was well advised
and to it all he gave consent.

[153]

He left her glad and gladly went.
Each one in bed throughout the night
remained awake and took delight
in thinking what seemed best to do.
As soon as they arose, the two,
who knew that they must be alone,
5230   deliberated on their own;
of each one's counsel they conversed.
Cligès recounted, speaking first,
what he had thought of in the night.
"My lady, what I think is right:
we can't do better, I believe,
than go to Britain and to leave.
To take you there is what I thought.
Don't make my planning come to naught!
Despite the greatness of the joy
5240   when Helen was received in Troy,
once Paris brought her as his choice,
far greater joy would people voice
throughout the king my uncle's land*
on your account, when we two land.
If you do not approve of it,
tell me what you consider fit,
because, whatever may occur,
I'll heed your counsel and concur."
She answered him: "I shall declare
5250   I never shall go with you there,
for if for Britain we were bound,
they'd talk of us the world around
like Tristan and Isolde the Fair,
once we had made our journey there,
and here and there all would proclaim
our rapture was a cause for blame.
None would believe, nor should they do,
that what has happened could be true.

Who would believe I could evade
your uncle and remain a maid?   5260
They would believe me light and lustful
and you a fool to be so trustful.
But the commandment of Saint Paul
is good to keep and to recall.*
Whoever will not keep him chaste
Saint Paul instructs to act with taste
and in a manner so discreet
he is not blamed for his deceit;
no outcry or reproach is flung.
It's wise to still an evil tongue.   5270
If it would not cause you distress,
I think I can achieve success;
I shall feign death and dead shall seem.
That is my thinking and my scheme.
A sudden illness will consume
my body, which you entomb.
Think carefully what we will need
and take the utmost care and heed
that tomb and coffin in its breadth
are built to keep me safe from death   5280
or suffocation from bad air,
and so no one becomes aware
when you come back at night to save
and take me from my sheltering grave.
Let none but you see where I hide;
allow no other to provide
what I may need or want myself,
save you, to whom I grant myself.
I won't accept in my life's span
the service of another man.   5290
You'll be my servant and my friend.
Whatever you do I shall commend.
No empire's lady shall I be

[155]

unless you are its lord with me.
Above these halls I'll rate a pallid

5296   and dismal place that's dark and squalid

a   when you are with me in that place.

b   If I have you and see your face,

c   I'll be a lady wealthy grown,

d   and all the earth shall be my own.

5297   If we behave with taste and sense,
no harm will come of our pretense.
None can reproach us; empire wide,

5300   all will believe that I have died,
and I am rotting in the earth.
My governess reared me from birth;
on Thessala I much rely;
trustworthy help she will supply.
I place great trust in one so wise."
Cligès so heard his friend advise.
"Thus, if we can achieve success
and you believe your governess
has counsel that is sound and fair,

5310   all to be done is to prepare,
my lady, and we must be fleet.
If we aren't prudent and discreet,
we're bound to meet complete disaster.
I have a craftsman who's a master
and sculpts with an amazing hand,
a carver known in every land
for work that he has done and made
and sculpted, modeled, and portrayed.
He is my serf; his name is John.*

5320   If he is willing to take on
some complex project or rendition,
he simply has no competition.
Mere novices are all the rest,
like infants at the nurse's breast.

The men of Rome and Antioch
have used his works and made a mock*
to learn what they know how to do,
but no one knows a man more true.
Now I shall test him with the plan,
if he should prove a loyal man,   5330
to set him free and all his heirs.
I'll never catch him unawares
by keeping back what you propose,
if he vows never to disclose
my doings, by the pledge he made,
and swears to give me loyal aid."
"Therefore so be it," she replied.
Cligès took leave and went outside.
On the departure of Cligès,
Fenice sent for her governess,   5340
whom she'd brought from her native land.
When she had spoken her command,
thence Thessala came straightaway
and did not tarry or delay;
why she was summoned was unknown.
She asked the empress, when alone,
what was her pleasure and her will.
Not holding back or keeping still,
Fenice detailed her full intent.
She said, "Nurse, I am confident   5350
whatever things I may declare
you will not let be known elsewhere.
I've often put you to the test;
your wisdom leaves me much impressed.
You've done so much, I love you so;
I turn to you in every woe.
No other counsel do I take.
You well know why I lie awake
and what I wish for and devise.

[157]

5360 I can see nothing with my eyes
except the one thing that I treasure,
but I shall never have my pleasure
without first paying very dear.
Yet I have found my match and peer,
for, if I want him, he wants me,
and if I suffer, so does he
from my own suffering and pain.
Now I must tell you and explain
my thinking and my conference
5370 and what decisions made good sense
that we two reached upon our own."
Fenice informed her and made known
that her intention was to feign
an illness, bitterly complain,
and end by dying of her plight.
Cligès would steal her off that night.
"We'll be together from that day."
She felt there was no other way
she would be able to endure.
5380 If Thessala could reassure
Fenice that she would lend her aid,
they would perform this death charade
and know that nothing would go wrong.
"My joy and fortune are so long
in coming and are so far distant."
In all she would be her assistant,
her governess was very clear
Fenice should never doubt or fear.
She'd labor for her benefit,
5390 and once she put her hand to it,
it would appear to anybody
Fenice's soul had left her body.
So all with certainty would think
once that she gave Fenice a drink,

a beverage that would make her frigid
and pale and colorless and rigid;
her breathing and her speech would fail,
yet she would be alive and hale,
for good or ill, sensationless,
immune to harm or to distress   5400
for one day and one full night's gloom
within the coffin or the tomb.
Fenice said, fully made aware,
"My lady, I am in your care
in everything that you may do.
I'm not superior to you.
Now I am yours, take care of me
and tell these people whom I see
that every single one must go.
I'm ill, and they distress me so."   5410
So Thessala began to tell
the lords, "My lady is unwell,
and she requests you to withdraw.
Your loud talk makes her nerves feel raw,"
she told them with all courtesies.
"She will not rest or be at ease
while in this chamber you remain.
I've never heard her so complain
of any malady before,
and thus I am concerned the more.   5420
Don't be annoyed, but take your leave.
Please do not speak with her this eve."
At her instruction, off they went.
Meanwhile Cligès in private sent
for John to come from where he stayed.
Thus was his secret offer made:
"John, guess what I am putting forward?
You are my serf; I am your lord.
Mine to dispose by sales or cessions,

5430 to use your body and possessions
in any way I feel inclined.
I have an enterprise in mind.
If you can prove your loyalty,
forevermore you would be free,
and so would all your heirs as well."
John instantly began to tell,
desiring greatly to be freed:
"Sir, as you wish, we are agreed.
A task that makes me free for life
5440 and frees my children and my wife
is one to which I'll put my hand.
Thus you must tell me your command,
for nothing is too difficult.
What toil and effort may result
will never make me discomposed,
though, if I said I was opposed,
I'd have to do it nonetheless
and put aside my business."
"True, John, but this is an affair
5450 I dare not tell unless you swear
and give your pledge and surety
in all ways of your loyalty.
Pledge you will help with my concern
and not let anybody learn."
"Sir, very willingly," said John.
"And never doubt me thereupon;
my oath and promise I now give
that never, all the days I live,
will I say one thing I believe
5460 would trouble you or make you grieve."
"John, should I suffer martyrdom,
there's none to whom I'd dare to come,
save you, whose counsel I would try.
5464 I would prefer to lose an eye.

It would be better I were slain   a
than tell another or explain,   b
but you are so discreet and true   c
I'll tell you what I mean to do.   d
I think that you will do my will,   5465
and both assist me and keep still."
"Sir, that is true, God grant me aid."
Cligès detailed the plan he made.
Once that the truth had been disclosed,
to which you all have been exposed,   5470
for you have heard me tell the plan
and well know what he told his man,
John told Cligès he could be sure
that John would build the sepulcher
as perfectly as he could make.
John told Cligès he wished to take
Cligès with him to see a house
none of his children or his spouse
had ever seen, one known to none.
He'd show Cligès what he had done   5480
and bring Cligès to where John hewed
and carved in total solitude;
none of his workmen had been there.
He'd seen no place more fine and fair
than was the one John wished to show.
Cligès responded, "Then let's go!"
Below the city, far remote,
his labors well deserving note,
John built a tower with skillfulness.*
John took him there and led Cligès   5490
through its apartments to acquaint
Cligès with images in paint
with which they were illuminated,
where rooms and fireplaces awaited.
John led Cligès both up and down

[161]

this dwelling place remote from town
where no one lived and no one went;
Cligès inspected its extent.
From one room to the next he passed
5500   until he thought he'd seen the last.
The tower was pleasing, good and fair.
The maid would live in comfort there
for all her days, he told John so,
and nobody would ever know.
"It never will be known, my lord,
the joys my whole tower may afford.
Do you think all have been revealed?
Some places are so well concealed
they can't be found by any man.
5510   To prove it, search as best you can.
You can search everywhere forever,
and so can others, wise and clever,
and won't find more apartments here
unless I make their presence clear.
Know I have not failed to acquire
all that a lady would require.
For her to come is our sole care,
because this tower is a fair
and comfortable place to be.
5520   This tower, as you well can see,
has been built wider at the base.
You'll find no doorway anyplace
or entryway in any part.
By such ingenious skill and art
the door is made out of hard stone;
you'll never find the join alone."
"I have heard wonders," said Cligès.
"I'll follow you with eagerness
to see what things may be ahead."
5530   John took Cligès's hand and led

the way until they came before
a smoothly finished, polished door
with paint and color overall.
At that John leaned against the wall.
By the right hand he led Cligès.
He told him, "Sir, no man can guess
there is a window or a door
within this wall that we explore.
Do you see any way to manage
to pass through it avoiding damage?"   5540
Cligès replied that he saw none
and would not think it could be done
unless he saw. Yes, John replied,
he'd open up the doorway wide.
John, who had done this work before,
unlocked and opened that wall door;
no harm or damage did he do.
In single file they passed on through,
went down a spiral stair, and halted
in an apartment that was vaulted,   5550
where John would do the work required
on any project he desired.
"Now, here we are, sir," John relayed.
"Of all the men God ever made
we two alone have been in here,
and yet, as shortly will be clear,
this place is comfortable and sweet,
so let this place be your retreat.
Conceal your friend here thus recessed.
Such lodgings well suit such a guest,   5560
for rooms and hot baths can be found,
hot water piped from underground.
Whoever felt that it was meet
to find a comfortable retreat
to place and keep his friend concealed

would have to go quite far afield
to find a place as fit and right.
Sir, you will find it a delight,
once you have been all through the place."
5570 John showed him all built in that space.
"John, my own friend," Cligès decreed,
"both you and all your heirs are freed,
and I am totally your own.
I want my love here, all alone,
with none to know she's past this door
save you and me and her, no more."
John said in answer, "I thank you!
Now here we have no more to do.
We've been here long enough today;
5580 let us go back without delay."
"You've spoken well," Cligès replied.
"Let's go." They went back and outside,
and from the tower they exited.

THE EMPRESS'S ILLNESS

IN town they heard, as people said
to one another, spreading word:
"Something amazing has occurred
to lady empress, did you hear it?
That wise good lady? Holy Spirit
grant her good health, if so He will,
5590 for she is lying very ill."
On hearing rumor and report,
in haste Cligès went back to court;
no joy or bliss was to be had,
for everyone was crushed and sad.
The empress made them so, who feigned;
the illness of which she complained

[164]

did not cause her distress or smart.
She said she hurt in head and heart.
This illness had so strong a hold,
none could come to her room, she told,   5600
save king or nephew, either man.
Those were the two she dared not ban,
but if her lord the emperor
did not come through her sickroom door,
she did not care. Since she had placed
herself in peril and she faced
great pain by reason of Cligès,
his absence caused her much distress.
She wished to see no one but him.
Cliges, within the interim,   5610
would come to her and would expound
upon the things he'd seen and found.
He came before her to report;
the time he stayed was very short.
Fenice, so people would believe
what pleased her rather made her grieve,
cried: "Go away, oh, go away!
You bother me with what you say!
I feel so dreadful, rest assured
that I shall never rise up cured."   5620
Cligès, well pleased this was the case,
departed, pulling a sad face.
You never would see one so drear.
Though sad outside might he appear,
his heart was gay in counterpoise,
anticipating future joys.
The empress had not fallen ill
but played ill while complaining still.
The emperor raised loud lament,
believed her ill, for doctors sent.   5630
By doctors she would not be seen

[165]

and would not let them intervene
or let herself be touched or pressed.
It made the emperor distressed
when she announced in her condition
she never would consult physician,
save one who knew the way with ease
to give her health when he might please,
for he would make her live or die.

5640   On him she freely would rely
for health and life. The other folk
believed it was of God she spoke
and failed to grasp what she made known,
because she meant Cligès alone.
He was her god who could supply
a cure for her or make her die.
The empress would not give permission
for scrutiny by a physician.
She would not eat or drink, so vivid

5650   her ruse, till she turned pale and livid
just to deceive the emperor worse.
She was attended by her nurse,
who'd searched with an amazing guile
throughout the city's bounds meanwhile,
so no one had the least idea,
to find a potful of urea
of a doomed woman none could treat.
Just to improve on this deceit,
she paid her visits to assure

5660   the woman she could work a cure
and promised she would use her skill.
She brought this woman who was ill
a urinal, came to collect
her urine daily, which she checked,
until the woman was past hope,
beyond all medication's scope.

That day would be the woman's last.
The urine that the woman passed
she guarded and did not disclose
until the emperor arose.   5670
She went at once with: "Sire, command
your doctors all to be at hand.
My lady, ill as she can be,
would now have your physicians see
this specimen, but make it clear
before her they may not appear."
Within the hall came each physician.
They saw the urine's bad condition.
Each said, so they were in accord,
that she would never be restored   5680
or live until midafternoon,
or, if she did so, late or soon,
the Lord would gather home her soul.
So these physicians as a whole
agreed on as they whispered low.
The emperor gave them to know
the truth of it they must dispense.
They said they had no confidence
at all in her recovery,
and she would not survive past three.   5690
By then she would give up the ghost.
When he had heard what they prognosed,
it all but felled the emperor.
He nearly swooned upon the floor,
and so did those he was amid.
No people mourned the way they did
throughout the palace on that morning.
I shall omit the words of mourning.
But Thessala now worked as mixer
and brewer of the drugged elixir.   5700
She stirred and pounded what she brewed,

for, long ago, she had accrued
all the ingredients she knew
would be required to make the brew.
When it was nearly on the brink
of three, she gave Fenice the drink.
Once she had drunk, it blurred her sight.
Her face became as pale and white
as if she had been bled. The potion
5710   so worked that there was not a motion
of hand or foot she could contrive,
not if she should be flayed alive.
She did not budge or say one word,
and yet she understood and heard
the emperor's lament and all
the cries and wails that filled the hall.
Throughout the city people swept
and made this outcry as they wept:*
"Lord, we are stricken and heartsore,
5720   all on account of Death, that whore.
Death, you are evil, covetous,
unheralded, invidious,
insatiable of appetite.
You could not take a meaner bite
out of the world that is around you.
What have you done, Death? God confound you!
What total beauty you've suppressed.
For what was holiest and best
(had she lived) that God used His skill
5730   to strive to make is now your kill.
God was too patient and too fair
when He gave you the power to tear
His things to pieces as you've done.
In your battalion you are one
whom God in wrathfulness should bar,
because you have gone much too far

in your outrageous insolence."
Thus all the people took offense
and wrung their hands and beat their palms.
The clerics prayed and read their psalms   5740
for their good lady, to cajole
God to have mercy on her soul.
Amid the tears and wails and cries,
the written text so testifies,
out of Salerno* there came three
physicians, who were elderly,
(they had stayed in that town for long).
They asked of the lamenting throng,
because they stopped to hear the woe,
what sorrow caused the tears to flow.   5750
What made them crazed with grief and cry?
Some persons told them in reply:
"Lord, don't you know why, gentlemen?
Because the whole world would have been
crazed with us, in a steady path,
if it but knew the grief and wrath
and loss and damage and dismay
that we have suffered on this day.
Good Lord, from what place have you come
to this town's pandemonium,   5760
not knowing what has just occurred?
We want to let the truth be heard,
because we want you three to share
the grief and sorrow that we bear.
Don't you know Death, with her grim pall,
desiring all and seeking all,
who everywhere lurks for the best,
as is her custom, has distressed
our city with a crime today?
God sent one brightness, one light ray,   5770
and thus He made the whole world shine.

[169]

Death cannot alter her design
or keep from doing as she likes,
and ever in her power she strikes
the very best that she can find.
To show her power unconfined,
she took one body and bereft
the world of more good than she left.
If Death took all the universe,
5780   she could not have done any worse.
The beauty, wisdom, courtesy,
and every splendid quality
that any lady could display
cheat Death has stolen all away;
all virtues that were once possessed
by lady empress Death suppressed
and thereby slew us without pity."
"Oh, Lord, how you detest this city,"
said the physicians, "to be sure,
5790   since we were not here earlier.
If we had come the day before,
Death could have felt superior
if she stole anything from us."
"Physicians were so odious
to her, my lady would not see
or let you treat her malady.
We've many good physicians here.
My lady would not let one near;
she would see none and never pleased
5800   to let one treat her when diseased.
Not for the world would she have done."
The doctors thought of Solomon:
such hate his wife exhibited
she tricked him by appearing dead.
This lady might have done the same.
But if they could, by any claim,

get in to her to treat her case
and of deceit found any trace,
for no man born would they tell lies
but tell the truth without disguise.   5810
At once to court the doctors went,
where there was noise and such lament
God's thunder was inaudible.
The senior man, most knowledgeable,
went straight up to the coffin's side,
and no one pulled him back or cried,
"Don't touch her!" The physician pressed
his hand upon her side and breast
and knew without a doubt her soul
was still within her body, whole.*   5820
He clearly saw the emperor,
who came to him and stood before,
near slain by sorrow and appalled,
so this physician loudly called:
"Now, emperor, I bring relief.
Be comforted; in my belief
this lady surely is not dead.
Leave off your grief; be comforted.
If I don't bring her back again,
then you can have me hanged or slain."   5830
Immediately the noise that filled
the palace quieted and stilled.
The emperor told the physician
he could command with free volition
whatever he would have him give
if he could make the empress live,
but if instead they were bereft,
he'd have the doctor hung for theft
if he had told the slightest lie.
The doctor said, "I shall comply.   5840
"If I don't make her speak to you,

[171]

for mercy I shall never sue.
Clear out this palace and proceed;
don't give it any thought or heed;
allow nobody to remain.
What malady has caused her pain
I must examine on my own.
These two physicians, these alone,
who are associates of mine,
5850   may stay with me, as I assign,
and all the others must be gone."
Cligès and Thessala and John
would have opposed the doctor's plan,
except, if they opposed the man,
all people present in that throng
would have been sure to take it wrong.
Discreetly, they made sure to laud
what they heard others there applaud;
out of the palace they all went.
5860   The three physicians roughly rent
the lady's shroud, which was not clipped
with scissors or a knife but ripped.
They told her, "Do not be afraid,
my lady, or become dismayed.
Speak in complete security.
We all perceive with certainty
you are completely sound and well.
Cooperate, be sensible,
and do not give way to despair.
5870   If for our counsel you would care,
we three all promise we will do
5872   all in our power in helping you;
a   whether it be for good or ill,
b   we will be loyal to you still,
c   both in concealment and in aid.
d   Long arguments need not be made,

for you can make entirely free   e
with all of our ability,   f
and therefore you should not refuse."   5873
Thus they endeavored to confuse,
deceive, and trick her, but in vain;
since she did not wish to obtain
the service that their promise meant,
the doctors' efforts were misspent.
When those physicians saw they were
obtaining no response from her,   5880
for all that they might coax and ask it,
they took Fenice out of the casket
and said if she'd not speak again,
she'd swiftly think herself insane.
The horrors she would undergo
would be untold and ones that no
poor women's body had endured.
"We all are certain and assured
you are alive and do not deign
to speak to us but rather feign   5890
to play false with the emperor.
You must not fear us anymore.
If someone's given you offense,
before we do you violence,
disclose what you intend to us,
for you are being odious.
We will assist you, nonetheless,
from wisdom or from foolishness."
It could not be; it was no use.
Then the physicians tried abuse   5900
and with their whips launched an attack,
so welts appeared all down her back.
Her soft flesh was so badly whipped
that they drew blood, which oozed and dripped.
When they had whipped and cut her flesh

until they brought blood flowing fresh
and running down as it escaped
from bloody welts and wounds that gaped,
they still had no results thereby:
5910   they did not wring one word or sigh,
nor did they make her move or stir.
They said that they required for her
both fire and lead, which without qualms
they'd melt and pour into her palms
before they'd let her fail to speak,
and fire and lead they went to seek.
They lit the fire to melt the lead.
The villains dealt abuse this dread
to hurt the lady: when they got
5920   the lead they melted boiling hot,
the way they took it from the brands,
they poured it in her open hands.
They were not even satisfied
the lead passed through from side to side,
so that her palms were pierced right through.*
The worthless bastards said anew
if she did not cease keeping still,
next they would put her on a grill
until she turned into a roast.
5930   But she kept still without riposte
through beatings and abuse so dire.
They meant to put her on the fire
so they could roast and grill her frame,
and then some thousand ladies came.
They parted from the crowd, came back,
and, through the doorway's tiny crack,
saw how the lady was ill used
and being horribly abused
by the physicians as a whole,
5940   who'd placed her over flame and coal

[174]

so they could torture her the more.
In order to break down the door
they ordered ax and hammer brought.
They caused great noise and great onslaught.
The door was shattered and then breached.
If these physicians could be reached,
they would receive without delay
their just desserts in every way.
Thereon, into the palace rushed
the ladies, all together, crushed,   5950
and Thessala was in the crowd,
her sole concern to be allowed
to reach her lady, whom she viewed
beside the fire, completely nude,
as she was left abused, abased.
Back in the coffin she replaced
and wrapped her in the shroud anew.
The ladies went to give their due
and set the three physicians straight.
They did not send for or await   5960
the emperor or seneschal.
They threw them out the windows, all;
down to the courtyard ground they crashed,
so that all three physicians smashed
necks, ribs, arms, legs when down they fell.
No ladies ever did so well.
Most hideously in this way
the three physicians drew their pay,
because the ladies paid their due.
Cligès felt great dismay and rue   5970
when he had heard and realized
how his sweetheart had agonized
for him from torture of such kind.
He very nearly lost his mind
for, rightly, he was filled with dread

[175]

she might be crippled, maimed, or dead
from agony and martyrdom
caused by those doctors who had come,
and so he anguished, overwrought.
5980   Then Thessala arrived and brought
a precious ointment she applied
with gentleness to wound and side,
a treatment that she went about
where her hurt lady was laid out.
In cloth of Syria, white of hue,
face bare, they wrapped Fenice anew.
The ladies' cries did not abate
that whole night long or terminate.
Throughout the town laments were raised,
5990   and by their grief they all were crazed,
highborn and low and rich and poor,
so it appeared each one made sure
to outdo all in cry and moan
and would not leave off on his own.
All night there were loud cries of mourning.
John came to court the following morning.
The emperor had sent to ask,
request, and order this new task.
"If ever, John, your work was skilled,
6000   use craft and knowledge now to build
a sepulcher, so none can find
another one so well designed."
Since he had done so, John declared
that he already had prepared
a finely carved and splendid tomb,
although he only could presume,
at the endeavor's origin,
none but a saint would lie therein.
"Instead of relics," John proposed,
6010   "now let the empress be enclosed

within the shrine that I shall bring.
I think her a most holy thing."
"Well said," the emperor averred.
"The empress is to be interred
at Lord Saint Peter's monastery.
With corpses in its cemetery
she is to be interred outside,
for she begged me before she died
to let it be her resting place.
Go now and choose the finest space   6020
and seal the tomb that you erect,
as is both fitting and correct,
on fairest burial ground for her."
John said in answer, "Gladly, sir."
Then John went swiftly with good will,
and he prepared the tomb with skill,
experience, and due regard.
Because the stone was very hard,
and more because the cold was dread,
within he placed a featherbed   6030
and scattered leaves and flowers meant
to give the tomb a pleasant scent.
More so, the flowers and the green
would keep the featherbed unseen
he'd placed within the sepulcher.
Each church and parish held for her
a service that was now all said.
Bells tolled, as fitting for the dead.
They had the body brought and laid
within the sepulcher John made   6040
and labored on so long and hard,
entombed within the burial yard.
The tomb was opulent and noble.
No one in all Constantinople,
though great or lesser, failed to go

[177]

behind the corpse, in tears and woe.
They cursed at Death and hurled complaints,
and knights and youths collapsed in faints,
and maids and ladies beat their breasts
6050   and pounded fists against their chests,
and they reproached Death as they wept.
"Ah, Death, why did you not accept
some ransom as my lady's price?
We felt her a great sacrifice,
while she meant little gain to you."
Cligès was crazed with grief and rue
more than the rest, in dreadful state,
his lamentation was so great.
By his own hand he might have died,
6060   but he postponed his suicide
until the hour he could exhume
and hold the lady in the tomb
and learn if she still lived to save.
The barons gathered at the grave
and placed and laid the body there,
but left the work, as John's affair,
of settling the tomb in place.
They could not see inside the space;
all fell and fainted, for good measure,
6070   and therefore John had ample leisure
to do his work with none to fret.
He got the sepulcher well set;
without assistance he disposed
the tomb, which he sealed, joined, and closed.
A person could feel proud of heart
to open and to take apart
whatever John had joined and fit
and not break it or damage it.

FENICE was in the tomb, sealed tight,
until the onset of dark night, 6080
with knights to guard her, thirty men,
and burning candles numbering ten
gave brightness and illumination.
The knights were worn by lamentation;
the weariness they felt was great,
and so that night they drank and ate,
until, together, they all slept.
Cligès stole off that night and crept
from court and all its retinue.
Of knights and men-at-arms, none knew 6090
the least about where he had gone.
He kept on till he came to John,
who counseled him as best could be.
He furnished him with weaponry,
which never would be necessary.
The two spurred toward the cemetery
in arms but found the burial ground
enclosed by high walls all around.
The sleeping knights within were sure
that they had made the place secure. 6100
From inside they had closed the gate
so nobody could penetrate.
Cligès did not know what to do
about a way of passing through.
Though entry through the gate was barred,
he must get in the burial yard.
Love urged and told what that entailed:
the graveyard wall he sought and scaled,
for he was bold and moved with ease.
Within there was a grove of trees, 6110

a planted orchard;* therewithal
one tree was planted near the wall,
and over it the branches grew.
Cligès had what he wished in view;
he used that tree and down he slid.
The very first thing that he did
was opening the gate for John.
They saw the knights all sleeping on,
and therefore they put out the light,
6120   so not a gleam remained to sight.
John was uncovering the grave
and opening the tomb and gave
no mark to it as he exhumed.
Cligès climbed down and disentombed
his friend and carried her outside,
so limp, it seemed that she had died.
He hugged her, though he did not know
if he had cause for joy or woe;
no speech or movement came from her;
6130   and John reclosed the sepulcher
and worked as fast as he could do
so there was not the slightest clue
that anyone had touched the place.
Then for the tower they set their pace
as swiftly as they had the power
and, when they put her in the tower
down in the chambers underground,
removed the shroud that wrapped her round.
Cligès, who had not any notion
6140   her body still contained a potion
and it had made Fenice become
completely motionless and dumb,
believed therefore that she was dead,
and he despaired, discomfited,
and wept and heaved a heavy sigh.

Meanwhile the time was drawing nigh
to when the potion's force would wane.
Fenice, who heard Cligès complain,
began to struggle, when she heard,
to comfort him by look or word.   6150
As for her heart, it all but broke
to hear lamenting that he spoke
the while she strove to intervene.
He said: "Ah, Death, you are so mean!
When things grow old and past all care,
those you reprieve and those you spare.
To live and last they are consigned.
Death, you are drunk, out of your mind,
to slay my love in place of me.
It is a wonder that I see: 6160
My love is dead and I'm alive.
Sweet friend, why does your friend survive
and see you lying dead this way?
Now everyone may rightly say,
since in my service you have died,
that I have caused your homicide.
Then I have been Death all along
who murdered you—is that not wrong?
Then of my life you are deprived;
I took your life when I survived,   6170
for weren't your health and life my weal,
sweet friend, a joy that I could feel,
and weren't my health and life your own?
I loved no one but you alone;
therefore the two of us were one.
It is my duty I have done:
Your soul is now within my frame,
and from your corpse my own soul came,
and our souls should keep company
each where the other soul may be   6180

and never should be separate."
She sighed, "Friend, friend," in weakened state,
"I have not given up the ghost
entirely, but I have almost."
She whispered in the negative:
"Friend, I no longer wish to live.
I meant to act a part and feign
but have good reason to complain.
Death did not like the part I play;
6190   I may not live to get away.
The doctors' injuries I've borne,
who left my flesh cut up and torn.
But, nonetheless, if it could be
my governess could come to me,
she would make me completely hale
if effort were of some avail."
"You must not be concerned, my dear,
for I shall bring her to you here,"
Cligès said, "by this evening's end."
6200   "Let John fetch her instead, my friend."
John went to seek the governess
until he found her and could stress
he wanted her to come away
and on no pretext to delay.
Fenice was with Cligès; both were
within a tower awaiting her.
Fenice was in great need of care,
so badly hurt the nurse must bear
both ointment and electuary.
6210   Fenice would die were she to tarry
and a swift cure were not begun.
So Thessala began to run;
with balm and plaster she purveyed
electuaries she had made.
Then Thessala joined up with John.

Straight to the tower they went anon
and left the city, well concealed.
Fenice believed that she was healed
once she could see her nurse appear,
she trusted and held her so dear.   6220
Cligès said, "Welcome to the place,"
and greeted her with an embrace.
"You have my love, nurse, and esteem!
Now you must tell me how you deem
this maiden's wounds. How do you feel?
Do you believe that she will heal?"
"Without a doubt, sir, rest assured.
I shall have her completely cured
and healed within a fortnight's spell.
I shall make her so very well   6230
her health and spirits at that time
will never have been more sublime."
Then Thessala thought out her cure,
and John departed to procure
all things the tower ought to hold.
About the tower Cligès was bold
as to and fro he went and came.
He put a goshawk there, to claim
he went to see the molting bird.
His visits to the tower recurred.   6240
No other reason was made known
except the goshawk, that alone.
Both night and day at any hour
he stayed and had John guard the tower;
against his will none entered it.
No illness pained Fenice a bit,
Thessala's cure was salutary.
He'd not have thought a hawthorn berry
of dukedoms, even the idea
of Morocco, Tudela, Almería,*   6250

[183]

compared with joys that he could taste,
and Love indeed was not debased
when those conjoined he had combined.
It seemed to one another's mind,
upon exchanging hug and kiss,
the whole world, through their joy and bliss,
became much better than before.

6258   Now do not ask me any more.
a   But everything that each might want
b   the other would approve and grant,
c   and thus their common will was done
d   as if the two of them were one.
6259   For that whole year and much of next,
6260   three months and more, if I'm correct,
Fenice remained within the tower.
The summer came, and leaf and flower
burst forth on trees, and small birds voiced
the joy they felt as they rejoiced
in language special to each bird,*
and then Fenice one morning heard
the nightingale in song. Cligès
was holding her with gentleness,
one arm at neck and one at waist;
6270   Fenice held him likewise embraced,
and then she started to contend:
"How good for me, my dearest friend,
would be a garden filled with trees
where I'd take pleasure at my ease.
For months, more than a full fifteen,
no sun or moonshine have I seen,
and, if there could be any way,
I'd gladly go outdoors by day.
I am enclosed within this tower.
6280   If, nearby, I could seek a bower
for recreation in the wood,

it would do me a world of good."
Cligès avowed that he would hear
John's counsel once he saw him near.
Immediately John came in view,
because, as was his wont to do,
he came and went with frequency.
Cligès informed him what would be
the thing for which Fenice had pled.
"It all is ready now," John said,   6290
"whatever it is she requires.
What she commands and she desires
this tower amply can provide."
Well pleased, Fenice asked John to guide
and to escort her to the site.
He answered, "Just as you think right."
John went to open up a door,
of which I cannot tell you more,
not how that door would be portrayed,
what kind it was, how it was made.   6300
It could be made by John alone,
and no one other could have known
a door or window was concealed.
While shut, it would not be revealed.
Fenice beheld the door ajar,
and sunlight burst in from afar,
which she had long not seen emerge.
Her blood pulsed with a joyous surge.
She needed but to be exposed
to open air while thus enclosed;   6310
she did not wish to live elsewhere.
She found an orchard, very fair,
and entered with delight and glee.
Its center held a grafted tree
with flowers laden, and which spread
its leafy branches overhead.

[185]

The boughs were trained so that they hung
down toward the ground and curved and swung
to near the earth, all bent thereto,
6320   save for the trunk from which they grew.
The trunk grew straight up from the base.
(Fenice could want no other place.)
Beneath the tree the lawn had grown;
fair and delightful it was shown.
Though hot the summer sun might be
when highest over that canopy,
the rays of light could not pass through,
so well John managed it and knew
the way to guide and train the boughs.
6330   For pleasure, there Fenice would drowse
and have her bed beneath the tree.
There they had joy and ecstasy.
A lofty wall enclosed the bower
on every side, joined to the tower,
so nothing else could enter there,
unless it climbed the tower stair.
Fenice had nothing to displease
or irk her and was well at ease
when under flower and under leaf;
6340   her every longing found relief;
her lover oft in her embrace.
In hunting season, people chase
with pointer and with sparrow hawk
and hunt wild duck and lark and stalk
the quail and partridge when they bird.
A knight from Thrace, as it occurred,
a lord of youthful energy
and well esteemed for chivalry,
whose name was known to be Bertrand,
6350   came very near the tower land
when he went out to hunt one day.

His sparrow hawk had flown away,
for it had sought and missed a lark.
Bertrand would think his fortunes stark
to lose his hawk while at the chase.
The orchard at the tower base
was where the sparrow hawk alit.
Bertrand was very pleased by it;
he thought his hawk would not be lost.
He strove to scale the wall and crossed   6360
the top and managed to get in.
He saw together, skin to skin,
beneath the grafted tree, at peace,
Cligès in slumber with Fenice.
"Lord, what is happening to me?
What is this wonder that I see?
Is that Cligès? Yes, that is so.
Can he be with the empress? No.
None more like her could one suppose;
she has the forehead, mouth, and nose   6370
my lady empress had alone.
Until now, Nature has not known
the way to duplicate two creatures.
I see my lady in her features;
no differences can I derive,
and were the empress still alive,
I should say truly, it is she."
A pear fell down out of a tree
and landed near Fenice's ear.
She wakened with a start of fear   6380
and saw Bertrand and cried with dread:
"My friend, my friend, now we are dead.
Bertrand is here. If he escapes,
we'll fall into a trap that gapes.
He'll say he's seen us and will tell."
At that Bertrand perceived as well

[187]

she was the empress, without doubt,
and found it crucial to get out,
because Cligès had brought his blade
6390 within the orchard and had laid
the sword before him while he slept.
He picked the sword up as he leapt.
Bertrand took flight, began to climb
and nearly scaled the wall in time,
for he was nearly over it
when by Cligès Bertrand was hit
with upraised sword and forced to flee,
his leg cut off below the knee,
sliced like a stalk of fennel plant,
6400 so hard a blow Cligès did plant.
Bertrand still managed to escape,
but crippled and in dreadful shape.
When people on the other side
beheld him, they were horrified;
their grief all but drove them insane
to see him suffering so much pain.
They asked Bertrand who did this deed.
He told them: "Put me on my steed
and do not question anymore.
6410 First I'll inform the emperor,
or else it never will be told.
The man should not be overbold
who did this injury to me.
He is in mortal jeopardy."
They put him on his palfrey's back,
and then, appalled by his attack,
they led him on his city route,
some twenty thousand in pursuit
accompanying them straight to court.
6420 The people coming to report
ran there pell-mell, without restraint.

For all to hear, Bertrand's complaint
had been made to the emperor,
but all thought him a troubadour
for telling tales that he had viewed:
the empress lying wholly nude,
with knight Cligès for company,
beneath an orchard's grafted tree.
Some people thought it was absurd.
The city in an uproar heard   6430
the news of which it was apprised.
To seek the tower, some advised
the emperor, would be the best.
Tumultuously, people pressed
with outcries at the emperor's side.
They found the tower unoccupied,
because Fenice left with Cligès
and Thessala. The governess
gave comfort and spoke reassurance
that if they saw, by chance occurrence,   6440
some other people coming there
who followed to arrest the pair,
the couple had no cause to fear;
these people could not get as near
to hinder them in their pursuit
or do them harm as men could shoot
strong crossbows with a winch's power.
The emperor came to the tower
and sent for John to come around.
He ordered him detained and bound   6450
and said that he would have him hung,
burned, and his ashes strewn and flung
for causing him humiliation.
John would receive his compensation,
a worthless one, for what he did,
for in the tower walls John hid

[189]

his wife and then his nephew too.
John answered, "What you say is true.
"I shall not tell lies or withhold
6460   whatever facts you would have told.
Moreover, if I have transgressed,
6462   I should be placed under arrest;
a   but since I wish to be excused,
b   I say no serf should have refused
c   whatever his true lord commands,
d   and everybody understands
e   that I am his; the tower is his."
f   "That it is not, John, yours it is."
g   "Mine? He first claims it, then I can.
h   I am not even my own man,
i   and I own nothing personally
j   unless he's granted it to me,
k   and if you are prepared to claim
l   my lord has wronged you and earned blame,
m   he need not order my defense
n   of him against your arguments.
o   But that gives me the hardiness
p   to tell you all and to express
q   my will and speak my mind to you
r   the way that I have worked it through,
s   because I know that I must die,
t   so come what may come by and by,
u   for if I die for my lord's case,
v   I shall not perish in disgrace.
w   The oath and pledge you gave your brother
x   is known to all, one and another,
y   that after you the emperor
z   would be Cligès, who's left our shore
aa   for exile; if it be God's will,
bb   he shall become the emperor still.
cc   Thus you deserve a reprimand.

You ought to seek no woman's hand   dd
and yet you married nonetheless   ee
and by your marriage wronged Cligès.   ff
Of wrongs toward you he was devoid,   gg
and if for him I am destroyed,   hh
if wrongly I draw my last breath,   6463
if he lives, he'll avenge my death.
So do the best that you can do;
if I die of it, you'll die too."
Rage caused the emperor to sweat
when he had heard this spoken threat
and grasped the point that John had made.
He said, "Your punishment is stayed   6470
until your lord's discovery;
he has proved treacherous toward me,
when I was so benevolent.
To cheat him was not my intent.
You will be held in prison, John,
and if you know where he has gone,
say so at once; I order it.
John answered, "How could I commit
a crime so treacherous and shoddy?
Should you draw my life from my body,   6480
I surely would not tell to you
my lord's location, if I knew,
especially now, God grant me aid.
I do not know for where they've made,
no more than you, upon this earth.
Your jealousy is of no worth.
I do not fear your anger so
as not to tell you all I know
about how you have been deceived,
although I shall not be believed: 6490
Your wedding day, you drank a brew,
and since it has deluded you.

No matter how your wife had seemed,
unless you were asleep and dreamed,
you never have had joy of her.
The night would make your dreams occur.
In dreams, such pleasure you could take
as if, when you were wide awake,
the empress held you in her arms.
6500   You had no other of her charms.
Her heart was so set on Cligès
that she assumed her deathlikeness
and she feigned dying for his sake.
Cligès informed me of this fake,
such trust in me did he accord.
My house, of which he is true lord,
is where he put her. Don't blame me;
Cligès, my own lord, may claim me.
If he gave orders which I spurned,
6510   I rightly should be hanged or burned."
The emperor began to think
about the brew he'd loved to drink,
so Thessala caused his deception.
Such thinking caused his first perception
that no enjoyment had he known
of his own wife except alone
the joy he'd savored while he dreamed,
enjoyment that was false, it seemed.
If he did not avenge the shame
6520   the traitor brought upon his name
when he absconded with his wife,
he'd have no joy throughout his life.
"As far as Pavia, instantly,"
he said, "from there to Germany,
begin the search and hunt him down
in every city, castle, town,
and any person on their track

who captures both and brings them back
I'll cherish more than any man.
Now search with all the care you can.   6530
Seek near and far and high and low."
They all set off when told to go
and searched the whole day, as assigned.
Cligès had friends there of a kind
who would prefer, if he were found,
to lead him to much safer ground
and not attempt to bring him back.
They spent two whole weeks on their track
and hunted them with pains and care.
But Thessala, who led the pair,   6540
brought them so safely from those parts
by her enchantments and her arts
they did not fear, upon their course,
the emperor and all his force.
The couple would not lie them down
within a city or a town
yet had whatever they might want
as much or better than their wont.
For anything the couple sought
was found by Thessala and brought.   6550
They all went back and left the chase.
Cligès went seeking at swift pace
his uncle Arthur, who was king,
until he found him and could bring
complaint and protests that he bore
against his uncle emperor,
who had most treacherously been wed
to leave him disinherited,
when he should not have wed a wife;
he'd pledged to take none all his life   6560
by his oath to Cligès's father.
He'd take a fleet, replied King Arthur,

to Constantinople for his rights
and fill a thousand ships with knights;
three thousand more ships with armed men.
Though strong and high they might have been,
each city, borough, castle, town
this army faced would be brought down.
Cligès made sure to thank the king
6570   for all the help he pledged to bring.
By royal summons, through his land,
all noble lords must come to hand.
He had men sent for to equip
bark, galley, cargo ship, and ship.
He had them fill three ships' expanses
with bucklers, armor, shields, and lances,
accoutrement well-armed knights wore.
The king made ready for a war,
his preparations were so vast
6580   that his arrangements far surpassed
both Caesar's and then Alexander's.
Throughout all England and all Flanders,
and Normandy, France, Brittany,
he summoned all the men that be,
as far down as the Spanish passes.
They were to cross the sea in masses,
when messengers arrived from Greece
to halt the passage for a piece,
before the king and men were gone.
6590   The messengers included John,
who was a most trustworthy sort,
who'd never witness or report
an incident that was untrue
or which he was not sure he knew.
The messengers were prominent
Greek citizens who had been sent
to find Cligès, searched all around,

[194]

and were elated he was found.
They said to him, "God save you, sire,
as in your empire all desire. 6600
Greece has been left you as your due,
Constantinople given you,
for both by rights are now your own,
because, which you have not yet known,
your uncle died of grief and pain
when he could not find you again.
His grief was such, he was deranged;
from food or drink he grew estranged,
so that he died a lunatic.
Dear lord, return now and be quick. 6610
Your barons sent along for you;
they all desire and long for you
and wish to make you emperor."
Some people heard what was in store
and happiness was what they felt,
while others would leave where they dwelt
and felt their pleasure would increase
to have the army go to Greece.
The trip was put off there and then.
Forthwith the king dismissed his men, 6620
and they disbanded and returned.
Cligès prepared in haste, concerned
with traveling to Greece again
and now unwilling to remain.
When once equipped, farewells he paid
both to the king and friends he'd made.
Then they set off; he took Fenice,
not stopping till they came to Greece.
The Greeks did properly accord
a joyous welcome to their lord. 6630
They gave his sweetheart as his bride
and crowned the couple side by side.

He made his sweetheart be his lady
and called her sweetheart, also lady,
so she lost nothing in the end.
He loved her as his own sweet friend;
she loved him with a love the same
as any sweetheart ought to claim.
Their love increased each day and grew;
6640   he never feared she was untrue
or to a quarrel felt disposed,
and she was never kept enclosed
as her successors were secluded.
Subsequent emperors concluded
wives should be feared, and all believed
that they might find themselves deceived
when they heard of the artifice
by which Fenice deceived Alis:
the brew he drank at his reception
6650   was first, and second the deception
that she had managed to envision.
As if the empress were in prison,
she is now kept in Constantinople,
no matter how high born and noble,
whatever her identity.
The emperor won't trust her free
while he recalls the other one,
and more from fear than from the sun,
he keeps her in a room secure.
6660   No male will ever be with her
unless a eunuch* since a lad.
With eunuchs no fears need be had
Love's bonds will ever bind such men.
Here ends the work of Chrétien.

NOTES

INTRODUCTION

1. Chrétien de Troyes, "Philomena and Procne," 200–279.

2. *New Arthurian Encyclopedia*, 37. Because of its reference to "le mal dagres" in v. 3849, Beroul's *Tristan* tends to be dated by the siege of Acre in the winter of 1190–1191.

3. Shirt, "How Much of the Lion," 1–17; Janssens, "Simultaneous Composition," 366–75.

4. Lejeune, "*Conte du Graal*," 65–67, 75.

5. Gerbert de Montreuil writes that Chrétien did not complete *Perceval:*

> Ce nous dist Crestiens de Troie
> Qui de Percheval comencha
> Mais la mors qui l'adevancha
> Ne li laissa pas traire affin . . .

[Chrétien de Troyes, who began the story of Perceval, told us this, but death, which overtook him, did not let him bring it to an end.] (Gerbert de Montreuil, *Continuation*, vv. 6984–6987, 214.)

6. The dates of Chrétien de Troyes's romances are disputed. Nitze proposes the earliest range of dates: after 1158 for *Erec and Enide;* after 1164 for *Lancelot;* around 1170 for *Yvain;* and before 1181 for *Perceval*, in *Perceval and the Holy Grail*, 284–85. The dates of 1170 for *Erec*, 1176 for *Cligès*, 1177 to 1179 or 1181 for *Yvain* and *Lancelot*, and after 1181 for *Perceval* are given by Frappier, *Chrétien de Troyes*, 9. Uitti with Freeman dates *Erec* 1165, *Cligès* 1176 to 1178, *Lancelot* and *Yvain* 1179 to 1180, and *Perceval* c. 1190, in *Chrétien de Troyes Revisited*, xiv. Luttrell proposes that Chrétien's romances were written during a shorter and later period between 1184 and 1190, in *Creation*, 32.

7. The love songs are entitled "Amors tançon et bataille" and "D'Amors, qui m'a tolu a moi." The latter song mentions the potion with which Tristan was poisoned. In both songs Love is personified as a masterful opponent. The songs are contained in Chrétien de Troyes, *Chansons courtoises*.

8. Mickel Jr., in "Theme," 52, states: "The debate over the authenticity of the work has raged since the mid-nineteenth century, with Foerster, Groeber, and Wilmotte arguing strongly in favor of the text's authenticity and Gaston Paris, Paul Meyer, and Jean Frappier voicing doubts and generally negative feelings about the quality of the *roman*."

9. Meade, *Eleanor of Aquitaine*, 129, 148.

10. Evergates, *Feudal Society*, 64, and Arbois de Jubainville, *Histoire*, vol. 3, 13, place the betrothal as early as 1148.

11. Luttrell notes that *Eracle* was begun by Gautier d'Arras for Countess Marie and her brother-in-law, Count Thibaut V of Blois, in *Creation*, 28.

12. See Arbois de Jubainville, *Histoire*, vols. 2 and 3, and Benton, "The Court of Champagne under Henry the Liberal."

13. His grandmother Adela (c. 1062–1137), countess of Blois, was the daughter of William the Conqueror and the sister of Henry I of England (1068–1135, r. 1100–1135).

14. Thibaut IV married Mathilda, the daughter of Engelbert, marquis of Istria and duke of Carinthia, from the outer boundaries of the Holy Roman Empire, the present-day Yugoslavia and Austria. Poinsignon, *Histoire générale*, 145, and Arbois de Jubainville, *Histoire*, vol. 2, 135–36, 260–64.

15. Through his mother's connections, Count Henri was involved in the negotiations between Frederick Barbarossa (c. 1123–1190, r. 1152–1190) and Louis VII regarding the election of Pope Alexander III in 1162 and was briefly the German emperor's hostage in 1163. See Arbois de Jubainville, *Histoire*, vol. 3, 47–63.

16. Benton, "The Court of Champagne as a Literary Center," 551–91.

17. Guillaume's youthful stay in England is mentioned by John of Salisbury, letter 307, in *Letters*, vol. 2, 746–47; Herbert of Bosham, epistola 5, *Patrologia Latina*, vol. 190, col. 1431; and the author of the *Book of St. Gilbert*, 176–79.

18. Bernard of Clairvaux protests youthful ecclesiastical honors for Guillaume in 1151 in a letter to his father, epistola 271, *Patrologia Latina*, vol. 182, col. 475–76. Thibaut ignored the saint's advice and made Guillaume canon of Cambrai and Meaux and provost of the chapters of Saint-Quiriace of Provins and of the cathedrals of Soissons and Troyes.

19. Guillaume negotiated with Henry II during his quarrel with his former chancellor and archbishop of Canterbury, Thomas à Becket, over the liberties of the English church. Guillaume was a regular visitor to Troyes, beginning in 1159, according to Benton, "The Court of Champagne under Henry the Liberal," 133.

20. John R. Williams, "William," 365–87.

21. Subsequently Guillaume became archbishop of Reims (1176) and cardinal of Santa Sabina (1179), regent of France (1190–1191), and head of the royal council of his nephew Philip Augustus. See *Gallia Christiana*, vol. 9, col. 95ff.

22. *Cartulaire*, vols. 1, 2. Representatives from Tironian abbeys and priories in Wales, Scotland, the Isle of Wight, and mainland England attended the annual general chapter at Tiron once every three years.

23. John of Oxenedes, *Chronica*, 270–71. In his foreword, xxxiv, Ellis states that John de Oxenedes, a monk of St. Benet of Holme, ends his chronicle in 1293. On page vii n. 2, Ellis notes: "There seems to have been a very early connexion between the

monastery of the Holme and St. Edmund's Bury." Hugh was castrated as a result of tensions in that war-torn region, an injury similar to the one of the Fisher King in Chrétien's *Perceval.*

24. Chertsey Abbey is on the Thames near London, outside Windsor Forest. Over a century later, in 1270, Chertsey Abbey prepared an exceptional set of tiles depicting the Anglo-Norman version of the Tristan legend by Thomas d'Angleterre (1170–1175). See Loomis, *Illustrations,* 14, and Shurlock, *Arthurian and Knightly Art.*

25. The annual fairs at Lagny, Troyes, Provins, and Bar-sur-Aube were supported and protected by the count of Champagne. The Lagny fair was on New Year's Morrow. The abbey of Lagny was heavily involved in it, and the fair revenues were important to the count of Champagne. See Bautier, *Economic Development,* 110–11.

26. In 1152 Hugh's father, Count Thibaut, died at Lagny, and his half brother Henri became count of Champagne and his half brother Thibaut V became count of Blois. Stephen died in 1154 and was succeeded by Henry II. In his *Chronicle,* 218–19, Robert de Torigni, the abbot of Mont St. Michel, states that Hugh returned to his brothers. Hugh returned to Champagne, and in 1156 Count Henri settled property on him at a Tironian priory near Epernay. See *Cartulaire,* vol. 2, charter 310, 83–84. Possibly Hugh traveled between his French possessions and his English abbey. He was elected abbot of Lagny with the support of Count Henri. See *Gallia Christiana,* vol. 7, cols. 497–98.

27. *Guillaume d'Angleterre,* v. 15.

28. See Frappier, *Chrétien de Troyes,* 237–40, and Foulet, "Appendix I," 288.

Tanquerey, in "Chrétien de Troyes," refutes the authorship. Holden, in "Géographie," 124–29, contends that the geography is invented. Robertson, in "Authorship," 158–60, takes a more nuanced position. Lonigan, in "Authorship," 308–14, comments on the love of parody and innovation common to the romances of Chrétien de Troyes. Mickel Jr., in "Theme," and Sturm-Maddox, in "'Si m'est jugie et destinee,'" 52–65, 66–80, are more supportive because of the shared religious themes. The familiarity of two brothers of Count Henri of Champagne with England, particularly Norfolk, furnishes additional support of Chrétien's authorship of *Guillaume.*

29. Lindvall, "Structures," 456–500, shows statistically that *Erec* and *Guillaume* are very similar in style and well below the average of complexity of Chrétien's romances. *Cligès, Lancelot, Yvain,* and *Perceval* are very similar in style and grouped well above the average of complexity.

30. The king of England was at Rennes in May 1169 and spent Christmas at Nantes. Warren, *Henry II,* 101, 110. See appendix, footnote 15. Also see Eyton, *Court,* 122–38. Laurie postulates that Chrétien was in Brittany in 1169 and 1170, attached to the English royal house, and that "the two young sons of Henri II, Geoffrey and the young Henry, may

have been Chrétien's charges, or at least informally in close contact with him in the Royal household, and his personal concern for them seems a genuine preoccupation," in "Chrétien de Troyes," 85–86. See also Carroll, "Quelques observations," 33–39. If Chrétien attended one of these ceremonies at Rennes, he may have visited the storm-making fountain in the nearby forest that Wace describes in *Roman de Rou*.

31. Bullock-Davies, "Chrétien de Troyes," 15, 25.

32. With regard to *Cligès*, vv. 1500ff., Bullock-Davies notes in "Chrétien de Troyes," 20–21, that King Arthur's army fords the Thames, and one part positions itself on the strip of low ground below the castle's north wall. The other part attempts to climb the slope to the castle but cannot scale the wall on the cliff. Count Angrès's men exit the old postern gate to the northwest and approach King Arthur's army from the edge of the chalk cliff. With regard to vv. 1708ff., she notes: "This means that four of the contingents advanced down the wooded slope leading from the lower or outer bailey, along the north front of the castle-wall facing the river and . . . through a cutting at the base of the cliff upon which the castle is built. Chrétien has described the site precisely." With regard to vv. 1849ff., she continues on page 23: "Chrétien knew the layout of the castle *within* the walls. . . . Alexander follows Count Angrès retreating along a hidden path, a narrow track leading to the top of the cliff and around the wall of the lower bailey, and follows him, passing through three walls from the lower bailey into the inner or upper bailey."

33. *Cligès*, v. 1047; Bullock-Davies, "Chrétien de Troyes," 14.

34. *Erec*, v. 6668; Schmolke-Hasselmann, "Henry II Plantagenet," 245, notes that Brian de Wallingford, also known as Brian Fitz Count, Brian de Insula, or Brian of the Isle, the natural son of Alain Fergent, count of Brittany, was the best friend of Henry II and helped him attain the English throne.

Cligès, v. 4543; Bullock-Davies, "Chrétien de Troyes," 27–29.

35. Book 6 of the *Metamorphoses* contains the stories on which *The Shoulder Bite* and *Philomena* are based, followed by the story of Medea and Jason in book 7.

36. See Curtius, *European Literature*, 68–105, and Faral, *Arts poétiques*, 48–54, for a discussion of rhetoric and topics.

37. Guyer postulates that Chrétien was listing his works in chronological order, in "Influence," 126–247. Gay counters his theory in "Chronology," 47–60, noting that *Erec and Enide* also contains references to the Tristan legend; hence Chrétien could have derived his Ovidian references, not from the Latin original, but from secondary sources such as the popular romances of the *Roman de Troie* and *Roman de Thèbes* and *Eneas*.

38. Hoepffner, "*Philomena*," 45.

39. Wace reproaches himself for his folly in visiting the fountain of Barenton to see whether it could cause rain:

> Fol m'en revins, fol i alai,
> Fol i alai, fol m'en revins,
> Folie quis, por fol me tins.

(Wace, *Roman de Rou*, vol. 3, vv. 6397–6398.) Chrétien repeats these lines in *Philomena*, vv. 503–504:

> Si m'an irai si con je ving,
> Ains mes por si fol ne me ting

and in *Yvain*, vv. 577–578:

> Ensi alai, ensi reving;
> Au revenir por fol me ting.

40. Schulze-Busacker, "*Philomena*," 478–79.

41. Fourrier dates Thomas 1172–1176, 1172 being the date when England seized Ireland, in *Courant réaliste*, 19–109.

42. The versions of *Cligès* that contain the *a mer*/*amer* pun and the *cors*/*cuer* dichotomy show that in the later romance Chrétien was influenced by Thomas. See Freeman, "*Cligès*," 106.

43. Arbois de Jubainville, *Histoire*, vol. 3, 71.

44. Munz, *Frederick Barbarossa*, 307–8. See also Uitti with Freeman, *Chrétien de Troyes Revisited*, 56–57, and Fourrier, *Courant réaliste*, 160–73.

45. Arbois de Jubainville, *Histoire*, vol. 3, 17.

46. Ehret, "*Passe avant le meilleur*," 155.

47. See note 39.

48. Brault, *The Song of Roland*, stanza 289, 240–43.

49. Frappier, *Chrétien de Troyes*, 110; Bullock-Davies, "Chrétien de Troyes," 32.

50. McCracken, "Women," 246, discusses Pliny's and Galen's accounts of herbs used to cause impotence and contemporary anesthetics based on mandragora. She also discusses urine analysis and reading of the pulse in medieval medicine (251).

51. See Verlinden, *Esclavage*, vol. 1, 396, 400–401, 838, and Huppert, *Black Death*, 112–16.

52. *Manuscrits*, ed. Busby et al., vol. 1, 13–14. See also Chrétien de Troyes, *Cligès*, ed. Micha, xviii–xx.

7. "*Commandments* Ovid once decreed" and *The Art of Love* are probably translations and adaptations of Ovid's *The Art of Love* and possibly *The Amores* and *Cures for Love.* See Ovid, *Erotic Poems.* These works by Chrétien have been lost.

The Shoulder Bite is a version of the story of Tantalus's son, Pelops, who was restored to life after being dismembered and served as a dish to the gods. Since one of the deities had taken a bite from Pelops's shoulder, the missing part was replaced with ivory. This story is in Ovid's *Metamorphoses,* book 6, vv. 403–411, 145. This work by Chrétien has been lost.

Chrétien's tale of King Mark and fair Isolde has been lost.

The metamorphosis of hoopoe, swallow, and nightingale is a version of Ovid's tale of Philomela or Philomena in *Metamorphoses,* book 6, vv. 424–674, 146–53. It immediately follows the story of Pelops, mentioned in note 2. *Philomena* is a tale of a sexual triangle between Tereus; his wife, Procne; and her sister, Philomena, who were changed into birds for their violent crimes. This work by Chrétien has survived. See Chrétien de Troyes, "Philomena and Procne," 200–279.

21. Beauvais, north of Paris, is noted for the lofty cathedral of St. Peter. Chrétien is claiming access to the library of the church of St. Peter, which burned in 1180.

42. Hunt notes in "Tradition" that the *translatio studii* topos (the passage of learning from the ancient to the modern world), "far from glorifying the ancient world, centres on France in modern times."

62. The Tristan legend begins with an account of the love and premature deaths of Tristan's parents, Rivalen and Blancheflor. See Bédier, *Romance,* 11–12. Chrétien similarly presents the love story of Cligès's parents, Alexander and Soredamors.

119. Clasping on the sword is part of the ceremony of knighting.

440. Prototypes of maidens who hold love in disdain include Lavine in the *Eneas* and Pomona in Ovid's *Metamorphoses,* book 14, vv. 623ff., 328–32.

453. The personification of love as a god named "Love" or "Cupid" armed with a bow and quiver of arrows is rooted in classical mythology and found in Ovid. See *Amores,* book 1, poem 1, vv. 21–25 (*Erotic Poems,* 86). Burrell notes in "Participation," 27: "Love, as it is in the *Eneas,* is an external, quasi-punitive, personified force which imposes itself from outside and governs the behavior of its host."

468. By including three long love monologues in this story of Alexander and Soredamors, Chrétien is verging on parody. There are precedents for this monologue in which love begins through betrayal by the eyes in Ovid's story of Narcissus (Ovid, *Metamorphoses,* book 3, vv. 339ff., 85–87) and of Medea and Jason (book 7, vv. 1–99, 155–58).

544. In a variation of this line, BN 375 reads: "Et amers est li maux ques tient" (And bitter sorrow do they see).

The pun in this manuscript with the Old French homonyms *la mer* 'sea,' *amer* 'to love,' and *amer* 'bitter' reflects Thomas's *Tristan*. See Benskin, Hunt, and Short, "Nouveau fragment," 289–319.

597. The comparison of secret love to fire under ashes is found in Ovid, *Metamorphoses*, book 4, vv. 63–64, 95–96.

618. In these love monologues the lovers engage in wordplay using the same vocabulary. Alexander's monologue picks up the key words of Soredamors's earlier monologue: "fool," "eyes," "heart," and "will." His monologue begins with "A fool . . ." and plays on the words "think," "pain," "health," "gracious," "game," "master" (in the sense of a schoolteacher), "arrow," "mirror," "glass," "candle," "rays," "friend," "enemy," and "gilt." Soredamors's next monologue also begins with "Fool . . ." and repeats "gracious," "friend," "will," "master," "eyes," and "gilt."

686. Alexander is debating with himself in the tradition of the schools. He refers to himself alternately as "I" and "you" as he poses and answers questions.

752. His "servants" are his heart and eyes.

762. The arrow is Soredamors.

838. By likening Soredamors's golden hair and head to the gilded feathers and nock of an arrow and having Alexander speculate about her clothed body as the hidden shaft of the arrow, Chrétien is inspired by Ovid, who refers to Phoebus's imagining the hidden charms of Daphne in *Metamorphoses*, book 1, v. 502, 42.

888. Guyer notes in "Influence," 128, that Soredamors's monologue may be compared to Medea's monologue in Ovid's *Metamorphoses*, book 7, vv. 11–73, 155–57.

1025. Soredamors's insomnia (vv. 868ff.) and her comment, "I've learned more than an ox of plowing!" are inspired by the passage in Ovid in which the insomniac narrator decides it is better to yield to love than to resist because "yoke-shy rebellious oxen collect more blows and curses than a team that's inured to the plough." *Amores*, Book 1, 2, vv. 13–14; see Ovid, *Erotic Poems*, 87.

1069. Ganelon betrays Roland in *Song of Roland*.

1243. Bullock-Davies notes that the wooden palisades were replaced by stone walls and the great stone tower was constructed between 1169 and 1178, in "Chrétien de Troyes," 14–16.

1345. A literary precedent for this fierce King Arthur is Charlemagne in *Roland*. A historical precedent is Henry II and his strong queen, Eleanor of Aquitaine. Guinevere keeps the king in negotiations over the captives' fate all afternoon, which is unlike the submissiveness she shows in *Lancelot*.

1423. This sentence seems to be inspired by the death of the traitor Ganelon. See Brault, *Roland*, stanza 289, vv. 3965–3974, 241–43.

1470. Bullock-Davies discusses this realistic description of a dry summer in England in "Chrétien de Troyes," 19–20.

1597. The theme of the hero rejoicing over strands of golden hair of his sweetheart is repeated in *Lancelot*, vv. 1354ff. Lancelot falls into worshipful ecstasy over some hair that Guinevere left entangled in an ivory comb by a fountain. Bédier, *Romance*, 72–75, recounts how Iseult sends Brangien to be murdered in order to conceal that Brangien substituted for her on her wedding night. Brangien confesses to the "crime" of having lent Iseult her white chemise for her wedding night because Iseult had torn her own white chemise during the voyage from Ireland, and her life is spared. Guinevere comes to her tryst with Lancelot, wearing a pure white chemise (*Lancelot*, vv. 4578). As in the Tristan legend, in *Cligès* and *Lancelot* the white chemise symbolizes the physical integrity of the lady.

1676. In *Roland* God makes the sun stand still to give Charlemagne more time to overwhelm the Saracens (Brault, *Roland*, vv. 2458–2459, 150–51.

1715. Bullock-Davies notes in "Chrétien de Troyes," 21: "Chrétien has described the site precisely."

1849. Bullock-Davies notes in "Chrétien de Troyes," 23–24: "Chrétien knew the layout of the castle *within* the walls. . . . Earlier, in v. 1233, he had noted the *two* walls and ditches which could be seen from the outside; here he has correctly added the *third* wall or rampart which divided the tower from the two baileys."

2339. The medieval theories of pregnancy, derived from Galen and Avicenna, postulated a union of male and female seed, which ripened into an infant. See Jacquart and Thomasset, *Sexuality*, 48–70.

2366. This passage recalls the shipwreck of the *White Ship* on 25 November 1120, with only one survivor. William Atheling, the only legitimate male heir of King Henry I of England, was drowned.

2502. The *Roman de Thèbes* (written around 1150) contains the story of the conflict between Polynices and Eteocles.

2652. Munz, *Frederick Barbarossa*, 308, notes that during a complicated power struggle between the German emperor Frederick Barbarossa and Pope Alexander III, who was supported by the Greek emperor Manuel Comnenus and the rebellious Lombards, "in June 1171, a Greek embassy had come to Cologne and returned to Constantinople, accompanied by an official German negotiator."

2685. The name Fenice recalls the phoenix, a symbol of the resurrection of Christ. The crucifixion symbolism is carried further in the heroine's torture, in which molten lead is poured through her palms, and her burial.

2727. In addition to the story of Narcissus in *Metamorphoses*, book 3, vv. 339–510, 83–87, Achilles likens himself to Narcissus in *Roman de Troie*.

2751. In Bédier, *Romance*, 13, the squire Gorvenal teaches Tristan to use lance, sword, and bow and the hunter's craft.

2793. Chrétien has resumed the wordplay on "will" of the earlier love monologues.

2966. The name "Thessala of Thessaly" evokes the story of Jason and Medea of Thessaly and her witchcraft in Ovid's *Metamorphoses*, book 7, vv. 1ff., 155–66. The treatment of her role as a childhood nurse to a lovesick heroine who promises to use medicine or sorcery to fulfill the heroine's passion for a man denied to her is also similar to the story of Myrrha and her nurse in Ovid's *Metamorphoses*, book 10, vv. 382ff., 235–37. Since Myrrha has conceived an incestuous passion for her father and Medea is a sorceress and a murderess, Chrétien is clearly implying that Fenice's love story has a sinister side. Thessala's role is also similar to that of Iseult's maid, Brangien, in the Tristan story, who helps her mistress avoid disgrace on her wedding night and administers the magic potion.

3109. Fenice's remarks against the adulterous passion of Tristan and Isolde seem to reflect Chrétien's support of love within marriage. Since Tristan is King Mark's nephew, his passion for his uncle's wife, his aunt by marriage, is incestuous. It is also a betrayal of the loyalty owed by vassal to liege lord. This passage indicates the anti-Tristan nature of *Cligès*.

3149. Fenice will indeed be buried alive (vv. 6040ff.).

3445. A bezant is a gold coin of the Byzantine empire.

3812. Many manuscripts give "turtledove," but "trout" in BN 1420 seems more likely to associate with beaver.

See Curtius, *European Literature*, 94–98, for the topos of the world upside-down.

3821. This passage refers to the possibly fictitious "courts of love" held by Countess Marie of Champagne and her mother, Eleanor of Aquitaine, who are later described by Andreas Capellanus as handing down verdicts on love problems submitted for their consideration.

3853. This *adynaton* is the topos of stringing together impossibilities. See Curtius, *European Literature*, 95–98.

4202. When gold was rubbed on a black touchstone, the color of the streak was used to determine the purity of the metal.

4276. The engagement took place in Regensburg, near the Danube and the Black Forest in present-day Bavaria. The wedding took place in northern Cologne. The imperial couple, returning to Greece via Regensburg, has just parted company with the German emperor. Near Regensburg, Cligès is not as close to Britain as he would have been in Cologne in modern western Germany, but he is much closer than he would be if he returned to Greece and Constantinople and set out again.

4353. This fear is literally a kite fear, the kite being a member of the hawk family.

4365. In her long love monologue, Fenice ponders the phrase "I am totally your own," which is given its full significance in *Lancelot* as expressive of the lovers' irrevocable commitment to one another. Her concern that Cligès may prove deceitful is shared by Medea in Ovid's *Metamorphoses*, book 7, vv. 39–41, 156.

4489. The meaning is a great show of oversolicitousness that the lord, upon rising, may have a bit of down from his pillow on his head. Ovid makes a similar recommendation in *The Art of Love*, book 1, vv. 150ff.: "If some dust should settle in your girl's lap, flick it away with your fingers; and if there's no dust, still flick away— nothing"; see *Erotic Poems*, 170. John of Salisbury discourses on the perniciousness of court flatterers in book 3 of *Polycraticus* (1159). See John of Salisbury, *Polycraticus*, 18–25.

4591. In his earlier romance, *Erec*, Chrétien includes long lists of warriors and heroes in the tradition of epics like the *Song of Roland*.

4610. Note that Gornemant of Gohort ranked fourth in *Erec* (v. 1675) and Sagremore was unranked (v. 1701).

4693. The place is literally Candia, which is in Crete.

4711. Lancelot and Perceval are the heroes of Chrétien's subsequent romances, *Lancelot; or, The Knight of the Cart* and *Perceval; or, The Story of the Grail*. Lancelot of the Lake first appears in *Erec*, v. 1674, ranked third behind Gawain and Erec.

4907. Since Sir Gawain is the brother of Cligès's mother, Soredamors, it would be awkward for Cligès to defeat his own uncle.

5243. In Ovid's *Heroides*, Paris assures Helen of her warm welcome in Troy; see book 16, vv. 175–186, 210–11. Again Chrétien links Cligès and Fenice with an ill-fated couple.

Technically, King Arthur is Cligès's great-uncle, for Sir Gawain, King Arthur's nephew, is Cligès's uncle. See also v. 6553.

5264. Chrétien is misquoting scripture, as he does in the prologue of *Perceval* when he attributes a verse from St. John to St. Paul. What St. Paul says (1 Cor. 7.9) is: "If they do not contain themselves, let them marry. For it is better to marry than to be burnt."

5319. Serf is usually understood to mean a peasant attached to the land and engaged in agriculture who owed certain dues and services to his lord and enjoyed certain rights, including marriage and enjoyment of the proceeds of his labor. In twelfth-century France, some urban serfs were professionals like bakers or blacksmiths but dependents of a lord who might transfer them with their dues and services to a monastery. In the twelfth century, some urban Greek slaves were craftsmen engaged in independent businesses. John enjoys great autonomy in the practice of his craft and is married, which is consistent with serfdom. Nonetheless, Cligès's entitlement to sell or transfer John's body and possessions and John's statement that he owns nothing personally suggest that Chrétien is portraying a slave of the Greek imperial family. John's serfdom borders on slavery.

5326. A mock is a copy to use as a pattern to imitate.

5489. In Thomas's *Tristan*, Tristan has a serf build a "salle aux images," or hall of statues, including one of Iseult, which he kisses and embraces. See Thomas of Britain, *Tristan*, 50–51.

5718. Chrétien has several love monologues earlier in *Cligès*, and here he presents three more laments on the cruelty of Death (see vv. 6047ff. and 6154ff.), in addition to the lament in vv. 2557ff.

5745. The medieval university of Salerno, Italy, was particularly noted for its medical school.

5820. The physician has taken her pulse.

5925. The scourging and perforated palms evoke the suffering of Jesus at his crucifixion.

6111. This orchard evokes the orchard in Bédier, *Romance*, 82–84, where Tristan and Iseult met and were spied upon by the dwarf Froncin.

6250. Tudela, in Navarre, and Almería, a southern Spanish port, were located in the Moorish kingdom of Spain.

6265. The line about the birds singing in their own language appears in *Yvain*.

6661. Ovid mentions a eunuch gatekeeper in *Amores*, book 2, 3; see *Erotic Poems*, 114.

BIBLIOGRAPHY

PRIMARY SOURCES

Andreas Capellanus. *The Art of Courtly Love.* Trans. John Jay Parry and ed. Frederick W. Locke. New York: Frederick Ungar, 1957.

Bédier, Joseph. *The Romance of Tristan and Iseult.* Trans. Hilaire Belloc. New York: Pantheon Books, 1945.

Bernard of Clairvaux. *Epistolae.* In *Patrologia Latina.* Vol. 182. Paris: Migne, 1879.

Béroul. *Le Roman de Tristan.* Ed. Ernest Muret. 4th ed. Classiques français du moyen âge 12. Paris: Champion, 1967.

The Book of St. Gilbert. Ed. Raymonde Foreville and Gillian Keir. Oxford: Clarendon, 1987.

Brault, Gerard J. *The Song of Roland: An Analytical Edition.* Vol. 2. Oxford Text and English Translation. University Park: Pennsylvania State University Press, 1978.

Bryant, Nigel. *The High Book of the Grail: A Translation of the Thirteenth-Century Romances of Perlesvaus.* Totowa, NJ: Rowman and Littlefield; Cambridge: D. S. Brewer, 1978.

Chrétien de Troyes. *Arthurian Romances.* Trans. William W. Kibler. London: Penguin, 1991.

———. *Arthurian Romances.* Trans. D. D. R. Owen. Everyman's Library. London: J. M. Dent, 1987.

———. *Chansons Courtoises.* Ed. and trans. Marie-Claire Gérard-Zai. In *Cligés,* trans. Charles Méla and Olivier Collet. Paris: Librairie Générale Française, 1994.

———. *Cligés.* Ed. Alexandre Micha. Paris: Champion, 1968.

———. *Cligés.* Ed. Stewart Gregory and Claude Luttrell. Cambridge: D. S. Brewer, 1993.

———. *The Complete Works of Chrétien de Troyes.* Trans. David Staines. Bloomington: Indiana University Press, 1990.

———. *Erec and Enide.* Ed. and trans. Carleton W. Carroll, with an introduction by William W. Kibler. Garland Library of Medieval Literature. New York: Garland, 1987.

———. *Erec et Enide.* Ed. Mario Roques. Classiques français du moyen âge. Paris: Champion, 1966.

———. *Guillaume d'Angleterre.* Ed. A. J. Holden. Textes littéraires français, no. 360. Geneva: Droz, 1988.

———. *Lancelot; or, The Knight of the Cart.* Trans. Ruth Harwood Cline. Athens: University of Georgia Press, 1990.

———. *Perceval; or, The Story of the Grail.* Trans. Ruth Harwood Cline. Athens: University of Georgia Press, 1983.

————. *Philomena.* Ed. C. De Boer. Paris: Geuthner, 1909.

————. "Philomena and Procne." In *Three Ovidian Tales of Love,* ed. and trans. Raymond Cormier, 200–279. New York: Garland, 1986.

————. *Yvain; or, The Knight with the Lion.* Trans. Ruth Harwood Cline. Athens: University of Georgia Press, 1975.

Gallia Christiana. Vol. 7. Paris: Ex Topographia Regia, 1744.

Garnier's Becket. Trans. Janet Shirley from the twelfth-century *Vie Saint Thomas le Martyr de Cantorbire* of Garnier of Pont-Sainte-Maxence. London: Phillimore, 1975.

Geoffrey of Monmouth. *Life of Merlin/Vita Merlini.* Ed. and trans. Basil Clarke. Cardiff: University of Wales Press, 1973.

Gerbert de Montreuil. *La Continuation de Perceval.* Ed. Mary Williams. Classiques français du moyen âge, no. 28. Paris: Champion, 1922.

Guillaume d'Orange: Four Twelfth-Century Epics. Trans. Joan M. Ferrante. New York: Columbia University Press, 1974.

Herbert of Bosham. *Epistolae. Patrologia Latina.* Vol. 190. Paris: Migne, 1854.

John of Oxenedes. *Chronica.* Ed. Henry Ellis. Vol. 13. Rolls Series. London: Longman, 1859.

John of Salisbury. *The Letters of John of Salisbury.* Ed. W. J. Millor, S. J. Brooke, and C. N. L. Brooke. Vol. 2. Oxford: Clarendon, 1979.

————. *Polycraticus.* Trans. Cary J. Nederman. Cambridge: Cambridge University Press, 1990.

Lancelot do Lac: The Non-Cyclic Old French Prose Romance. Vols. 1, 2. Ed. Elspeth Kennedy. Oxford: Clarendon, 1980.

The Mabinogion. Trans. Gwyn Jones and Thomas Jones. 2d ed. London: J. M. Dent, 1974.

Merlin: Roman en prose du XIIIe siècle. Ed. Gaston Paris and Jacob Ulrich. Vol. 2. 1886. Reprint, Paris: Firmin Didot, 1965.

Orderic Vitalis. *The Ecclesiastical History of Orderic Vitalis.* Vol. 6. Books 11, 12, and 13. Ed. and trans. Marjorie Chibnall. Oxford: Clarendon, 1978.

Ovid. *The Erotic Poems.* Trans. Peter Green. New York: Penguin Books, 1982.

————. *Heroides and Amores.* Trans. Grant Showerman. Cambridge, MA: Harvard University Press, 1977.

————. *The Metamorphoses.* Trans. Mary M. Innes. New York: Penguin Books, 1955.

La prise d'Orange. Ed. Claude Régnier. Paris: Klincksieck, 1967.

Le roman de Tristan en prose. Ed. Gilles Roussineau. Vol. 3. Geneva: Droz, 1991.

Thomas. *Les fragments du roman de Tristan.* Ed. Bartina Wind. Textes littéraires français, no. 92. Geneva: Droz, 1960.

————. *Tristan.* Ed. Stewart Gregory. New York: Garland, 1991.

Wace. *La partie arthurienne du roman de Brut*. Extract of manuscript BN, fr. 794. Ed. I. D. O. Arnold and M. M. Pelan. Bibliothèque française et romane, series B: Texts and documents 1. Paris: Klincksieck, 1962.

———. *Le roman de Brut*. Ed. Ivor Arnold. 2 vols. Paris: Société des Anciens Textes Français, 1938–1940.

———. *Le roman de Rou de Wace*. Ed. Anthony Holden. 3 vols. Société des Anciens Textes Français. Paris: A. and J. Picard, 1970–1973.

SECONDARY SOURCES

Altieri, Marcelle. *Les romans de Chrétien de Troyes: Leur perspective proverbiale et gnomique*. Paris: Nizet, 1976.

Arbois de Jubainville, H. d'. *Histoire des ducs et des comtes de Champagne*. Vols. 2, 3. Paris: Aug. Durand, 1860–1861.

The Arthurian Encyclopedia. Ed. Norris J. Lacy. New York: Garland, 1986.

Bautier, Robert-Henri. *The Economic Development of Medieval Europe*. London: Thames and Hudson, 1971.

Benskin, Michael, Tony Hunt, and Ian Short. "Un nouveau fragment du *Tristan* de Thomas." *Romania* 113 (1992–1995): 289–319.

Benton, John Frederick. "The Court of Champagne as a Literary Center." *Speculum* 36, no. 4 (October 1961): 551–91.

———. "The Court of Champagne under Henry the Liberal and Countess Marie." Ph.D. diss., Princeton University, 1959.

Bezzola, Reto R. *Les origines et la formation de la littérature courtoise en Occident (500–1200)*. Vol. 3. Geneva: Slatkine, 1984.

———. *Le sens de l'aventure et de l'amour (Chrétien de Troyes)*. Paris: La Jeune Parque, 1947.

Brogyanyi, Gabriel John. "Plot Structure and Motivation in Chrétien's Romances." *Vox Romanica* 31 (1972): 272–86.

Bullock-Davies, Constance. "Chrétien de Troyes and England." In *Arthurian Literature 1*, ed. Richard Barber, 1–61. Woodbridge, England: D. S. Brewer, 1981.

Burrell, Margaret. "The Participation of Chrétien's Heroines in Love's 'covant'." *Nottingham French Studies* 30, no. 2 (autumn 1991): 24–33.

Busby, Keith. *Gauvain in Old French Literature*. Amsterdam: Rodopi, 1980.

Carroll, Carleton W. "Quelques observations sur les reflets de la cour d'Henri II dans l'oeuvre de Chrétien de Troyes." *Cahiers de Civilisation Médiévale* 37 (1994): 33–39.

Cartulaire de l'Abbaye de la Sainte-Trinité de Tiron. Ed. Lucien Merlet. 2 vols. Chartres, France: Garnier, 1883.

Ciggaar, Krijnie. "Chrétien de Troyes et la 'matière byzantine': Les demoiselles du château de Pesme aventure." *Cahiers de Civilisation Médiévale* 32 (1989): 325–31.

Colby, Alice M. *The Portrait in Twelfth-Century French Literature: An Example of the Stylistic Originality of Chrétien de Troyes.* Geneva: Droz, 1965.

Curtis, Renée L. "The Validity of Fénice's Criticism of Tristan and Iseult in Chrétien's *Cligés.*" *Bibliographical Bulletin of the International Arthurian Society* 41 (1989): 293–300.

Curtius, Ernst Robert. *European Literature and the Latin Middle Ages.* Trans. Willard R. Trask. New York: Harper and Row, 1963.

De Lage, G. Raynaud. "Le procédé de la 'correctio' chez Chrétien de Troyes." *Boletin de Filologia* 19 (1960): 145–49.

Deroy, Jean. "Chrétien de Troyes et Godefroy de Leigni, conspirateurs contre la fin'amor adultère." *Cultura Neolatina* 38 (1978): 67–78.

Ehret, Henri. *"Passe avant le meilleur"; ou, L'histoire de ces comtes qui ont fait la Champagne.* Troyes, France: Renaissance, 1989.

Eisner, Sigmund. *The Tristan Legend: A Study in Sources.* Evanston, IL: Northwestern University Press, 1969.

Enders, Jody. "Memory and the Psychology of the Interior Monologue in Chrétien's *Cliges.*" *Rhetorica* 10, no. 1 (1992): 5–23.

Eskenazi, A. "Cheval et destrier dans les romans de Chrétien de Troyes (BN 794)." *Revue de Linguistique Romane* 53 (July–December 1989): 397–433.

Evergates, Theodore. *Feudal Society in the Bailliage of Troyes under the Counts of Champagne, 1152–1284.* Baltimore: Johns Hopkins University Press, 1975.

———. *Feudal Society in Medieval France.* Philadelphia: University of Pennsylvania Press, 1993.

Eyton, Robert William. *Court, Household, and Itinerary of Henry II.* London: Taylor, 1878.

Faral, Edmond. *Les arts poétiques du XIIe et du XIIIe siècle.* Geneva: Slatkine, 1982.

Field, P. J. C. "Malory and Chrétien de Troyes." *Reading Medieval Studies* 17 (1991): 19–30.

Flori, Jean. "Pour une histoire de la chevalerie: L'adoubement dans les romans de Chrétien de Troyes." *Romania* 100 (1979): 21–52.

Foulet, Alfred. "Appendix 1: On Editing Chrétien's *Lancelot.*" In *The Romances of Chrétien de Troyes: A Symposium,* ed. Douglas Kelly, 288. Lexington, KY: French Forum, 1985.

———. "On Grid-Editing Chrétien de Troyes." *L'Esprit Créateur* 27, no. 1 (1987): 15–23.

Foulon, Charles. "Les tendances aristocratiques dans le roman de *Guillaume d'Angleterre.*" *Romania* 71 (1950): 222–37.

Fourquet, Jean. "Le rapport entre l'oeuvre et la source chez Chrétien de Troyes et le problème des sources bretonnes." *Romance Philology* 9 (1956): 298–312.

Fourrier, Anthime. *Le courant réaliste dans le roman courtois en France au moyen âge.* Vol. 1. Paris: Nizet, 1960.

Frappier, Jean. *Chrétien de Troyes.* Paris: Hatier, 1968.

———. "Le motif du 'don contraignant' dans la littérature du moyen âge." *Travaux de Linguistique et de Littérature* 7, no. 2 (1969): 7–46.

———. *Le roman breton:* Cligés. Paris: Centre de Documentation Universitaire, 1951.

Freeman, Michelle A. "Chrétien's *Cligés:* A Close Reading of the Prologue." *Romanic Review* 67 (1976): 89–101.

———. "*Cligés.*" In *The Romances of Chrétien de Troyes: A Symposium,* ed. Douglas Kelly, 89–131. Lexington, KY: French Forum, 1985.

———. *The Poetics of Translatio Studii and Conjointure: Chrétien de Troyes's* Cligés. French Forum Monographs, no. 12. Lexington, KY: French Forum, 1979.

———. "Problems in Romance Composition: Ovid, Chrétien de Troyes, and the *Romance of the Rose.*" *Romance Philology* 30 (1976–1977): 158–68.

———. "Transpositions structurelles et intertextualité: Le *Cligés* de Chrétien." *Littérature* 41 (1981): 50–61.

Gay, Lucy M. "The Chronology of the Earlier Works of Chrestien de Troyes." *Romanic Review* 14, no. 1 (1923): 47–60.

Gregory, Stewart. "Fragment inédit du *Cligès* de Chrétien de Troyes: Le manuscrit de l'Institut de France." *Romania* 106 (1985): 254–69.

Guyer, Foster E. "The Influence of Ovid on Chrestien de Troyes." *Romanic Review* 12, nos. 2, 3 (1921): 97–134, 126–247.

Haidu, Peter. *Aesthetic Distance in Chrétien de Troyes: Irony and Comedy in* Cligès *and* Perceval. Geneva: Droz, 1968.

Holden, A. J. "La géographie de *Guillaume d'Angleterre.*" *Romania* 107 (1986): 124–29.

Holmes, Urban T., Jr. *Chrétien de Troyes.* New York: Twayne, 1970.

Hunt, Tony. "Chrestien de Troyes: The Textual Problem." *French Studies* 33 (1979): 257–71.

———. "Redating Chrestien de Troyes." *Bibliographical Bulletin of the International Arthurian Society* 30 (1978): 209–37.

———. "The Rhetorical Background to the Arthurian Prologue: Tradition and the Old French Vernacular Prologue." *Forum for Modern Language Studies* 6 (1970): 1–23.

———. "Tradition and Originality in the Prologues of Chrestien de Troyes." *Forum for Modern Language Studies* 8 (1972): 320–44.

Huppert, George. *After the Black Death.* Bloomington: Indiana University Press, 1986.

Jacquart, Danielle, and Claude Thomasset. *Sexuality and Medicine in the Middle Ages.* Trans. Matthew Adamson. Cambridge: Polity, 1988.

Janssens, Jan. "The Simultaneous Composition of *Yvain* and *Lancelot:* Fiction or Reality?" *Forum for Modern Language Studies* 23 (1987): 366–75.

Kelly, Douglas. *The Art of the Medieval French Romance.* Madison: University of Wisconsin Press, 1992.

———. *Medieval French Romance.* Twayne's World Author Series, no. 838. New York: Twayne, 1993.

———. "*Translatio studii:* Translation, Adaptation, and Allegory in Medieval French Literature." *Philological Quarterly* 57 (1978): 287–310.

Lacy, Norris J. *The Craft of Chrétien de Troyes: An Essay on Narrative Art.* Davis Medieval Texts and Studies, no. 3. Leiden, Netherlands: E. J. Brill, 1980.

Lacy, Norris J., Douglas Kelly, and Keith Busby, eds. *The Legacy of Chrétien de Troyes.* 2 vols. Amsterdam: Rodopi, 1987–1988.

Laurie, Helen H. C. R. "Chrétien de Troyes and the English Court." *Romania* 93 (1972): 85–86.

Lejeune, Rita. "La date du *Conte du Graal* de Chrétien de Troyes." *Le Moyen Age* 60 (1954): 51–79.

Levy, Raphael. "Old French Goz and Crestiiens li Gois." *PMLA* 46 (1931): 312–20.

Lindvall, Lars. "Structures syntaxiques et structures stylistiques dans l'oeuvre de Chrestien de Troyes." *Romania* 102 (1981): 456–500.

Lonigan, Paul R. "The Authorship of the *Guillaume d'Angleterre:* A New Approach." *Studi Francesi* 46 (January–April 1972): 308–14.

Loomis, Roger Sherman. *Arthurian Tradition and Chrétien de Troyes.* New York: Columbia University Press, 1949.

———. *Illustrations of Medieval Romance on Tiles from Chertsey Abbey.* Urbana, IL: University of Illinois, 1916.

Luttrell, Claude. "The Arthurian Traditionalist's Approach to the Composer of Romance: R. S. Loomis on Chrétien de Troyes." *Oeuvres et Critiques* 5, no. 2 (1980–1981): 23–30.

———. *The Creation of the First Arthurian Romance: A Quest.* Evanston, IL: Northwestern University Press, 1974.

———. "The Heart's Mirror in *Cligés.*" *Arthurian Literature* 13 (1995): 1–18.

Maddox, Donald. *The Arthurian Romances of Chrétien de Troyes: Once and Future Fictions.* Cambridge: Cambridge University Press, 1991.

———. "Trois sur deux: Théories de bipartition et de tripartition des oeuvres de Chrétien." *Oeuvres et Critiques* 5, no. 2 (1980–1981): 91–102.

Les manuscrits de Chrétien de Troyes / The Manuscripts of Chrétien de Troyes. Ed. Keith Busby, Terry Nixon, Alison Stones, and Lori Walters. 2 vols. Atlanta, GA: Rodopi, 1993.

McCash, June Hall. "Mutual Love as a Medieval Ideal." In *Courtly Literature: Culture and Context,* ed. Keith Busby and Erik Kooper, 429–38. Selected papers from the Fifth Triennial Congress of the International Courtly Literature Society, Dalfsen, Netherlands, 9–16 August 1986. Philadelphia, PA: John Benjamins, 1990.

McCracken, Peggy. "Women and Medicine in Medieval French Narrative." *Exemplaria* 2 (1993): 239–62.

McGrady, Donald. "The Hunter Loses His Falcon: Notes on a Motif from *Cligés* to *La Celestina* and Lope de Vega." *Romania* 107 (1986): 145–82.

Meade, Marian. *Eleanor of Aquitaine.* New York: Penguin Books, 1991.

Ménard, Philippe. "Le temps et la durée dans les romans de Chrétien de Troyes." *Moyen Age* 73 (1967): 375–401.

Micha, Alexandre. *"Eneas et Cligés."* In *Mélanges de philologie romane et de littérature médiévale offerts à Ernst Hoepffner,* 237–43. (Publications de la faculté des lettres de l'Université de Strasbourg.) Paris: Belles-Lettres, 1949.

———. *"Tristan et Cligés."* *Neophilologus* 36 (1952): 1–10.

Mickel, Emanuel J., Jr. "Theme and Narrative Structure in *Guillaume d'Angleterre.*" In *The Sower and His Seed: Essays on Chrétien de Troyes,* ed. Rupert T. Pickens, 52–65. Lexington, KY: French Forum, 1983.

Misrahi, Jean. "More Light on the Chronology of Chrétien de Troyes?" *Bibliographical Bulletin of the International Arthurian Society* 11 (1959): 89–120.

Munz, Peter. *Frederick Barbarossa.* Ithaca, NY: Cornell University Press, 1969.

Murray, Stephen. *Beauvais Cathedral: Architecture of Transcendence.* Princeton, NJ: Princeton University Press, 1989.

The New Arthurian Encyclopedia. Ed. Norris J. Lacy. New York: Garland, 1996.

Nitze, William A. *Perceval and the Holy Grail.* University of California Publications in Modern Philology, vol. 28, no. 5. Berkeley and Los Angeles: University of California Press, 1949.

Noble, Peter S. *Love and Marriage in Chrétien de Troyes.* Cardiff: University of Wales Press, 1982.

Ollier, Marie-Louise. "The Author in the Text: The Prologues of Chrétien de Troyes." *Yale French Studies* 51 (1974): 26–41.

———. *Lexique et concordance de Chrétien de Troyes d'après la copie Guiot, avec introduction, index et rimaire.* Montreal: Institut d'Etudes Médiévales, 1986.

———. "Modernité de Chrétien de Troyes." *Romanic Review* 71 (1980): 413–44.

Paris, Gaston. Review of Foerster edition of *Cligés,* by Chrétien de Troyes. In *Mélanges de littérature française du moyen âge,* ed. Mario Roques, 229–327. Paris: Champion, 1966.

Pickens, Rupert T. *The Sower and His Seed: Essays on Chrétien de Troyes.* French Forum Monographs, no. 44. Lexington, KY: French Forum, 1983.

Poinsignon, Auguste Maurice. *Histoire générale de la Champagne et de Brie.* 2d ed. Châlons-sur-Marne, France: Martin, 1896.

Polak, Lucie. *Chrétien de Troyes:* Cligés. Critical Guides to French Texts, no. 23. London: Grant and Cutler, 1982.

Ritchie, R. L. Graeme. *Chretien de Troyes and Scotland.* Oxford: Clarendon, 1952.

Robert of Torigni. *Chronicle of Robert of Torigni, Abbot of the Monastery of St. Michael-in-Peril-of-the-Sea.* In *Chronicles of the Reigns of Stephen, Henry II, and Richard I.* Rolls Series, vol. 82, no. 4. London: Longman, 1889.

Robertson, David W., Jr. "Chrétien's *Cligés* and the Ovidian Spirit." *Comparative Literature* 7 (1955): 32–42.

Robertson, Howard S. "The Authorship of the *Guillaume d'Angleterre.*" *Romance Notes* 4 (1963): 156–60.

Schulze-Busacher, Elisabeth. *Proverbes et expressions proverbiales dans la littérature narrative du moyen âge français.* Geneva: Slatkine, 1985.

Shirt, David J. "*Cligés:* A Twelfth-Century Matrimonial Case-Book?" *Forum for Modern Language Studies* 18 (1982): 75–89.

———. "Godefroi de Lagny et la composition de la *Charrette.*" *Romania* 96 (1975): 27–52.

———. "How Much of the Lion Can We Put before the Cart?" *French Studies* 31 (1977): 1–17.

Shurlock, Manwaring. *Arthurian and Knightly Art from the Middle Ages.* Ed. Derek Bryce. Restored designs by John Leb. Dyfed, England: Llanerch, 1989.

Stuard, Susan Mosher. "Ancillary Evidence for the Decline of Medieval Slavery." *Past and Present* 149 (1995): 3–28.

Sturm-Maddox, Sara. "'Si m'est jugie et destinee': On *Guillaume d'Angleterre.*" In *The Sower and His Seed: Essays on Chrétien de Troyes,* ed. Rupert T. Pickens, 66–80. Lexington, KY: French Forum, 1983.

Tanquerey, F. J. "Chrétien de Troyes, est-il l'auteur de *Guillaume d'Angleterre?*" *Romania* 47 (January–April 1931): 75–116.

Tichener, Frances H. "The Romances of Chrétien de Troyes." *Romanic Review* 16 (1925): 165–73.

Topsfield, L. T. *Chrétien de Troyes: A Study of the Arthurian Romances.* Cambridge: Cambridge University Press, 1981.

Uitti, Karl D., with Michelle A. Freeman. *Chrétien de Troyes Revisited.* New York: Twayne, 1995.

Van Hamel, A. G. "*Cligés et Tristan.*" *Romania* 33 (1904): 465–89.

Verlinden, Charles. *L'esclavage dans l'Europe médiévale.* Vol. 1. Brugge, Belgium: De Tempel, 1955.

Vitz, Evelyn Birge. *Orality and Performance in Early French Romance.* Cambridge: D. S. Brewer, 1999.

Walter, Philippe. *La mémoire du temps: Fêtes et calendriers de Chrétien de Troyes à la "Mort Artu."* Paris: Champion, 1989.

Walters, Lori. "Le rôle du scribe dans l'organisation des manuscrits des romans de Chrétien de Troyes." *Romania* 106 (1985): 303–25.

Warren, W. L. *Henry II.* Berkeley and Los Angeles: University of California Press, 1973.

West, G. D. *An Index of Proper Names in French Arthurian Verse Romances, 1150–1300.* University of Toronto Romance Series, no. 15. Toronto: University of Toronto Press, 1969.

Williams, Harry F. "The Authorship of *Guillaume d'Angleterre.*" *South Atlantic Review* 51 (1987): 17–24.

———. "Chrestiiens li Gois." *Bibliographical Bulletin of the International Arthurian Society* 10 (1958): 67–71.

Williams, John R. "William of the White Hands and Men of Letters." In *American Essays in Medieval History,* presented to C. H. Haskins, ed. C. H. Taylor, 365–87. Boston: Houghton Mifflin, 1929.

Woods, William S. "The Plot Structure in Four Romances of Chrestien de Troyes." *Studies in Philology* 50, no. 1 (1953): 1–15.